Items should be returned on or be
shown below. Items not alrea... ...ted by other
borrowers may b...   by
telepho...

ba

IT SHOULDN'T HAPPEN TO
A HAIRDRESSER

IT SHOULDN'T HAPPEN TO A HAIRDRESSER

Celebrity Tales From My Crimping Days

Steven Smith

The Book Guild Ltd

First published in 2011 by The Book Guild Ltd

Second edition published in Great Britain in 2017 by
The Book Guild Ltd
9 Priory Business Park
Wistow Road, Kibworth
Leicestershire, LE8 0RX
Freephone: 0800 999 2982
www.bookguild.co.uk
Email: info@bookguild.co.uk
Twitter: @bookguild

Cover photograph © www.jamiehughesphotography.com

Typeset in Garamond by Ellipsis Digital Limited, Glasgow

Printed and bound in the UK by TJ International, Padstow, Cornwall

ISBN 978 1912083 978

British Library Cataloguing in Publication Data.
A catalogue record for this book is available from the British Library.

To Lester Middlehurst

Contents

Foreword

Over the three decades I have known him, Steven has gone from crimping my hair in the salon to styling me for numerous newspaper and magazine shoots. But he's done much more than just make me look good – he makes me feel good too, as a true friend and someone who has always been there for me.

There's never been a dull moment in our 30-year friendship and Steven has had more reinventions than his idol Madonna! It wouldn't surprise me if, one evening, having poured myself a chilled glass of wine and settled back to watch *Coronation Street*, I suddenly saw him pulling pints behind the bar at The Rovers and shouting 'Any more for Betty's hotpot?' Actually, he'd probably be running the place.

I remember when he exploded onto television without warning, making me splutter over my morning cuppa as I heard his cheery 'Morning Lorraine' echo out from my TV set. 'So, my Steven's a TV hairdresser now,' I said to myself in amazement – and admiration.

Then there was the time he agreed to help out a journalist pal at *The Sun* who'd been let down by a no-show model for the Dear Deidre photo-problem feature. The title of the shoot – 'Jim's awkward problem' – should probably have sounded a warning bell for Steven but, always up for a challenge, he went ahead.

He kept it a secret though, so imagine the scene with me and my best friend Rose Hirst, relaxing by the pool on holiday in Tenerife, flicking through the back pages of *The Sun*. I still remember the shock of seeing my old mate stripped down to his underpants as his scantily-clad 'wife' in stockings and suspenders attempted to seduce him!

Rose and I collapsed into tears of laughter; we howled so much it became physically painful and in the end we were politely asked to leave the pool area because we were causing such a disturbance.

We could still barely speak when we rang Steven back in London. As always, he was happy to laugh at himself too and admitted he would be glad when the fuss died down, as he'd had burly men on building sites yelling at him all week. 'Oi, Jim, how's the problem?' But Steven is always game for a laugh.

After a hugely successful hairdressing career, Steven became a tabloid journalist, something I only realised when he sat down with his tape to interview me. When I asked him why, he simply replied: 'Felt like a change, darling,' throwing the usual sideways look he gives me when he thinks I might not approve. I have to say it felt odd having the man I know so well ask soul-searching questions that he already knew the answers to. But who could argue with his change in career when his writing has now been published all over the world?

Steven and I have globe-trotted together, as he has covered my holidays for a number of magazines, and he has added picture styling to his list of credentials. He ran the shoots with a military precision that made me nickname him 'Herr Flick', and I have to say it's the only time we really argue, as military precision is definitely not my thing!

He loves to tell the story of when he asked me get up at 4.30am so we could catch the best light for a beach shoot in Hurghada, Egypt. I (reluctantly) agreed and Steven promised me a coffee once we'd walked down to the beach and on the pier

I reminded him. He tells everyone it was a two-mile trek and that I behaved like a complete diva, but it was only a couple of minutes really. And I got my coffee although I was barely awake enough to drink it.

But there's never a dull moment when he's around and he even has my mum, Annie, in stitches. She worked with him on a shoot once and he teased her mercilessly – 'DO NOT eat that chip, Annie, you're not putting on weight on my shoot or you're off,' he told her, as she dissolved into giggles.

We don't live in each other's pockets but neither is ever far from the other's thoughts. Nothing could have brought us closer than the death last year of our dear friend, the showbiz journalist Lester Middlehurst. Much as Lester could be a royal pain in the ass, he was someone who was important to us both, and losing him has made us realise how precious friendship is. I am glad Steven's book is dedicated to Lester. It also doesn't surprise me that Steven, unlike so many others, has written his own book in his own words. If I were to hear him being interviewed on TV as a best-selling author, I wouldn't splutter into my coffee in surprise; I'd just think: 'That's my friend Steven. He's a star.'

Denise Welch

1

Exhibitionism Is a Drug

'Exhibitionism is a drug ... you get hooked!
I'm now taking doses that would kill a beginner.'
Quentin Crisp, *The Naked Civil Servant*

It is a warm, humid evening in California and I am truly glad to escape to my room at the Holiday Inn in Santa Monica. Feeling a little worse for wear, I lie down on the bed intending to have a good, long sleep. Just as I close my eyes, the phone rings and it's Helen Smith, the modelling agent. Helen always speaks nineteen to the dozen, as if she has been partying with Keith Richards, and midway through the stream of consciousness she suddenly blurts out: 'Why is her hair in bunches?' She is referring to her star client, the model Jordan, a.k.a. Katie Price, who has just been put under contract to *The Sun* newspaper.

Along with fashion editor, Sam Howard, and the celebrity photographer, Alan Strutt, I am in Hollywood shooting Jordan's first calendar. Jordan is getting ready to go out on the town with a rugby team she's met in reception, but still appears to have had time to call her agent to complain about the way I've done her hair on the beach that day. It is just the latest in a lengthy series of battles between me and the teenage glamour girl.

Thinking back to my first meeting with Katie, it was unusual anyway for me to have been called in as hair stylist on a Page

Three shoot. My normal role was to groom the hair of celebrities and models interviewed for *Sun* 'exclusives' or shoots for the 'Sun Woman' fashion section and makeovers on readers.

Stuart Higgins, the then editor of *The Sun*, had ordered a five-day 'Striptease' Page Three special, inspired by the Demi Moore movie. Each day, an item of clothing would be removed. As Demi was surprisingly unavailable, a Page Three girl had been brought in for the shoot instead.

The first day had already been shot and I knew something was up when I arrived at Click Studios at *The Sun*'s headquarters in Wapping. In a panic, Jan Wright, the self-appointed resident make-up artist, grabbed me and pulled me into the office. 'This new girl is very difficult,' she hissed. 'She didn't like the way I did her hair yesterday, but Stuart Higgins loves her.'

Jan then made an extraordinary request – she asked me not to do the girl's hair too well. It seems Jan had not had all the products she needed the day before, which is why the hair hadn't come out as well, and she didn't want to be shown up by me. Jan was in a state and it seemed the whole studio was in uproar over this demanding Page Three débutante.

In those days it was a cardinal rule that we never told anyone we worked on that Jan was in fact married to *Sun* photographer, Steve Lewis, who owned Click Studios and did most of the fashion and celebrity shoots.

I dragged my hairdressing bag through to the back changing rooms, followed by a frantic Jan. There, sitting on a stool and staring into the mirror, was the most stunning, fresh-faced beauty. She had curly hair and there was a bit of the tomboy about her but she really was a vision of loveliness. Until she opened her mouth, that is.

'You any fucking good?' she snapped, sounding as though she'd just come off a building site.

'I'm all right,' I laughed. My laughter was more to cover my embarrassment – I just wasn't used to women talking like that. Page Three girls I'd styled in the past, such as the ultra-professional Jilly Johnson or the charming Linda Lusardi, could burp and tell a dirty joke with the best of them, but would never have used such casual coarse language, particularly to someone they had just met. I have to admit I was a little shocked.

This might have been her first modelling job – she'd only just been taken on by the Samantha Bond agency – but there was nothing humble about Katie. Nor did she seem to suffer from any self-doubt. 'I am Jordan! All right?' she said, winking. As I started to scrunch-dry her hair, she carried on bossing everyone about, but there was something endearing about her. She certainly was a naturally beautiful looking woman.

As I finished drying her thick, curly hair, she turned to Jan. 'That's how it's supposed to look. You didn't have the right stuff,' she snapped. Katie was only about 18 at the time but she almost had the 40-something make-up artist in tears. I have to say, though, that this was one of only two occasions that Katie actually liked the way I styled her hair.

Once I got to know the new Page Three sensation, I realised that she was in fact quite shy and a typical Gemini. The heavier the make-up and the bigger the hair, the more Jordan would come out and Katie would be pushed into the background. The more shocking and badly behaved she was, the more attention she received; the public seemed to love the naughty girl act from the start. It swiftly became clear to me that Jordan was hooked on the drug of exhibitionism.

As she left the studio after that first shoot, we all looked at each other. Unlike most models, she had not removed the thick make-up before leaving and I was worried about her going out like that, particularly as it was the middle of the day and she was so young. But there was no telling Katie; she loved any attention.

3

After that first shoot, Jordan became an overnight hit, not just with the powers that be at *The Sun* but with the paper's millions of readers, who could not get enough of her.

Katie began to be booked not just for Page Three but also for fashion and editorial features. She always looked stunning – but I wonder what the readers would have thought if they could have heard her too. Not to put too fine a point on it, she had a mouth like a sewer. One of her favourite lines, after she'd had her lip make-up applied, was, 'What do you think of my cocksucking lips?' This she'd screech to the assembled crowd in the studio after blowing them a demure, lip-glossed kiss. 'How big's your packet, love?' was another of her raunchy conversation-stoppers. She once told me she saw no problem in looking at men's bulges, as men had stared at her boobs for years. 'It's all right though, Steve,' she said, giggling, 'I don't look at yours out of respect.'

She may have talked dirty, but in my time with her at least, Jordan was more ladylike than most when it came to sex and was certainly no slapper. She had a strict one-month rule before doing anything with a boyfriend; she enjoyed the flirtation and the attention she got during the chase.

It was a disastrous date with football star Teddy Sheringham that really helped Jordan secure her celebrity status. Sheringham agreed to go out with her after reading that he was her 'ideal man'. But word of the date leaked out and the story made it onto the front page of *The Sun*. The evening went horribly wrong anyway – in the flesh, Jordan was too much for the footballer, who told her to back off. But the front-page scoop was great news for Jordan's blossoming celebrity status and *Sun* readers lapped it up.

Keen to look her best for the evening, Katie had booked a private appointment with the fabulous make-up artist Sue Moxley, who worked at *The Sun* occasionally and now has her own column in the paper. At the studios a few days later, Katie confronted Sue, asking whether she had leaked the story. In fact Sue, who is now married to former Dollar singer David Van Day, would have been the last person in the world to leak a story, and it didn't take Jordan long to realise that too. But the make-up artist is still waiting for her fee for doing Katie's make-up that evening.

In those days I wished *The Sun* would take more of a shine to the lovely Kelly Brook. She did not do Page Three but had real star quality. I remember walking down King's Road with Kelly after styling her hair for a shoot with Formula 1 ace David Coulthard. She was everything that Jordan was not – charming and funny and sweet – and I told her that one day she would be a huge star. But it was Jordan who was put under contract to *The Sun*.

It was a constant battle with Katie over her hair. *The Sun* liked a clean, fresh look, while Jordan went for a more high glamour image. The brilliant photographer Jeany Savage did the pictures at *The Daily Star*. She had a great eye and was wonderfully skilled at bringing out the beauty in a woman. However, that did not suit *The Sun*'s preferred 'girl next door' look. When Melinda Messenger was put under contract to *The Sun*, Jeany did the first pictures, but features editor Sue Carroll ordered an immediate reshoot, as the hair and make-up were far too heavy.

On one job, Jordan arrived at Marylebone station with full make-up and her hair thickly greased down. 'This will do for the shoot,' she informed me. My friend Sam Howard, *The Sun*'s fashion editor, found Jordan amusing; I think she regarded the model as a naughty schoolgirl and, having been to an all-girls school herself, admired Jordan's cheek.

We were doing corset fashion and taking off to one of Henry VIII's old haunts to give the shoot a regal Tudor feel. But with Jordan looking the way she did, it threatened to turn into more of a Great Plague shoot! I had to wash Katie's hair but only had expensive conditioning shampoo with me. That would have taken hours to get rid of the thick grease so I opted instead to use the detergent-based shampoo at the hotel. Katie took instant offence at this, thinking I was taking the piss out of her and she barely spoke to me as I styled her hair.

She went on to do a great shoot, proving that as well as the topless work, she could do fashion photography. If only she could have managed to turn up with freshly washed hair, like most other models, then everyone's day would have been easier.

On the train back to London, Jordan was holding forth and her language became cruder and cruder. I was really embarrassed as people around us stared and whispered, so I reverted to sarcasm; being a Gemini myself I can understand dual personalities. This only made things worse. 'You have a bleeding strange sense of humour, you have,' she snapped, sinking back into her seat and becoming quieter for a brief moment.

I'm not sure where Katie gets it from but it's certainly not her mother. I met Amy Price when she came to the studio one day and she is charming and well mannered. I blow-dried her hair and, after I had finished, she grabbed my hand, saying: 'Look after my little girl. She will be all right, won't she?' So it clearly isn't a hereditary trait.

It became more and more difficult to try and determine what Jordan actually wanted done to her hair, which is naturally beautiful. She would talk about it being bigger, and adding pieces, so one day I decided to give her exactly what she wanted. After an hour of coiffing, we had it – the RuPaul/Cleo Rocos love-child look! But at last Jordan was happy with something I had done.

Katie actually enjoys looking like a drag queen. I recently saw Gary Cockerill, who is a very talented make-up artist, getting her ready and he must have put five hair pieces in, not to mention the false eye lashes. Later, on Channel 5 live, Katie took her make-up off – and looked ten times better. People on the make-up circuit joke that Gary only does the 'tranny' look and I think that's an unfortunate legacy of his experience with Katie. I've worked with him many times and the man is underrated.

The picture of Jordan's 'tranny' look appeared in *The Sun* on a Saturday and on Monday I had a call from a livid Helen Smith, Katie's agent. She blamed me and was on the phone for an hour, laying down the law on how Katie's hair was to look in the future. I barely got a chance to get a word in. But Jordan had only been holding bingo cards in the picture, for heaven's sake, and I honestly believed the photographer would send her back to be restyled once he saw what a fright she looked. Alas, he did not, and I took a lot of stick as a result.

Despite all that, I was asked to go to Los Angeles to do the hair for the first ever Jordan calendar. My invite owed more than a little to the fact that I managed to get Virgin airlines to sponsor the calendar. A few months earlier I had worked with the *Baywatch* public relations machine when it rolled into town, styling hair for Traci Bingham and the legendary David Hasselhoff among others.

Liam Hamilton from LWT, which aired the show, was a good friend and I suggested that we take Jordan on the *Baywatch* set. He liked the idea, as did senior executives at *The Sun* and so, after another long phone call from Helen Smith, I was packed and ready to go to LA.

Katie and I arranged that she would come to my flat in South Kensington and we would travel to Heathrow together for a lunchtime flight. She arrived on time and seemed very excited about the trip. As we waited for our car to arrive, I made her a cup of tea and she played with my dog Costa. She was really nice to me; this was the sweet Katie that you got a glimpse of on rare occasions, rather than the demanding Jordan who had all but taken over.

Alas, it didn't last long. Suddenly Jordan was back. 'I need my nails done before I get on the plane,' she snapped. But there was no time for a fresh set of acrylic nails to be applied and Jordan seemed confused as to why we could not just jump on a later plane while she had her nails attended to. I promised she could get them done as soon as we got to LA, soothing her by saying they were better at doing them over there anyway. She calmed down and got in the car and it was a relief when we arrived at Heathrow and met Sam Howard. Jordan was still obsessing about her nails though.

Sam and I were hoping we would all be upgraded to Upper Class but back then airlines were still fussy about how people looked. Jordan had her baps on show for all to see so we suggested that, just for check-in, she covered up. Boy, was that a mistake! You'd think we had asked her to cut her own leg off, the fuss she made. Eventually, though, she grudgingly agreed and we were duly upgraded. It didn't stop her throwing us a look that could have killed a man at a hundred paces.

Relaxing in Upper Class in the lounge was bliss – we were enjoying a drink and Jordan was at the other end of the room, playing some games. I heard some loud giggling and looked up, noticing that there was not a single straight man to be seen in the immediate vicinity. The giggling got louder and I went to see what was going on. I was greeted by quite a sight – Jordan on the ski machine in a tiny top and with her boobs bouncing up and down at a quite alarming rate. You've got to hand it to her: she knows how to please a crowd and she was, of course, surrounded by men.

On the plane Sam and I sat together with Jordan behind us. It was all quiet as we took off but the peace was shattered by Jordan's dulcet tones: 'OI! WHEN CAN YOU TAKE A PISS AROUND HERE?'

The trip had only just begun.

After clearing customs and getting our luggage, we were met

by Alan Strutt, who was already working out there. He and Sam went to get our hire car and Jordan and I sat chatting. As we talked, she turned back into Katie and, as she did, revealed a vulnerable side that had me really worried for her. 'Steve,' she said, 'how much am I getting paid a week from my contract with *The Sun*?'

I was truly shocked. Though today she presents herself as a canny businesswoman, at that time the poor love obviously didn't have a clue. Her agent Helen Smith – who later went bust, owing Katie a fortune – had not even told her what she was earning. Feeling for her, I gave Katie Sue Carroll's direct line at *The Sun* and told her to ask Sue. She might have been driving me mad with her behaviour and demands, but it was terrible to think that at the age of just 19 she was being taken advantage of. I remembered too how her mum Amy had asked me to look after her.

The next day, Alan Strutt took the car to do another shoot and was nowhere to be found. We spent most of the time getting Jordan's nails done, but she was not happy, and nor was Sam. Jordan expected *The Sun* to pay for her nails and Sam was in charge of the money. Even though Jordan did not like the way her nails had been done, she insisted on having acrylic put on her toes too and Sam picked the bill up.

After three days of Alan taking the car and disappearing to do other shoots, Sam put her foot down. Still, Alan insisted that he could shoot three fashion spreads and an entire calendar in just two days. I was forced to lie to my good friend Sue Carroll, whom I've known for 15 years, when she rang me to see how it was all going. 'Oh, great,' I said, reckoning there was no point in worrying her.

But then there was bad news from Liam Hamilton, who called me to say it was doubtful that LWT were taking *Baywatch* again and that David Hasselhoff had no time to see Jordan for at least two weeks.

I broke the news to Jordan and she was less than impressed. 'There's a surprise,' she said sarcastically, and turned her back. The implication was that I had made the whole thing up just to come on the trip.

There were more problems – despite California being such a liberal state, you cannot shoot topless on most of the beaches in LA. All shoots require a licence and we did not have one. This did not stop Alan Strutt though; he really can achieve in days what it would take other photographers months to do. He took us all to the naturist beach near Malibu and Jordan wore tiny little sparkly bikini bottoms. I put her hair in bunches, with matching hair band.

'You have to be bleeding joking,' she squealed. But Sam was happy and Alan thought she looked great and Jordan soon forgot about her hair as she clocked the action on the beach.

'OI YOU! GET YOUR TACKLE IN,' she howled at the top of her voice to one unfortunate sunbather.

'PERVERT! WHAT YOU LOOKING AT?' she screamed at another.

Her favourite way of addressing Alan Strutt was to yell: 'HEY, YOU PERVERT, WHEN YOU TAKING MY PICTURE?' Needless to say, most of the topless pictures were taken in the desert or a secluded area of the beach.

So, back to where I started: I am lying on my bed as Jordan gets ready for her date with the rugby team, listening to her agent going on and on about the bunches. She'd wanted her hair straight, she said – but what with the wind and the humidity, Jordan's hair would have curled up again no matter how many times I straightened it. I still have the bunches pictures and, to my eye, she's never looked lovelier.

Sam Howard agreed to chaperone Jordan with the boys and asked me to come too, at which point I start looking for a window to jump out of. Luckily, I get a reprieve and am allowed to give it a miss. The evening was a bit of a wash-out though – you have to be 21 to get into a bar and Katie was only 19 so that was a non-starter. That didn't stop Katie flirting so outrageously with the boys they thought they were onto a sure thing. Katie had to spend the night in Sam's room, as the boys kept calling her.

On the flight home, Jordan chatted with the cabin crew and after a bit she came giggling up to me. 'Oi! The crew think you and I were making a porn film in LA,' she shrieked at the top of her voice.

After that I did her hair a few times – though she always made it clear it was under protest – and saw her at the odd party or charity ball, where she would always be the focus of attention. I remember one evening at the 'Born Free' charity ball, when Jordan was dating the gladiator Hunter. I was there with Denise Welch and Denise was crying as they showed a sick lion suffering from distemper on the big screen. Denise nudged me to look over at Jordan, who was pouting and posing and oblivious to everything except for herself.

I did not see Jordan again for a few years but bumped into her again shortly after she had finished *I'm a Celebrity ... Get Me Out of Here*. I was with Sue Carroll and we were about to join Billy Murray, a great actor from *The Bill*, for dinner at Hell's Kitchen. Jordan was reporting on the show for ITV2, and as I walked down the red carpet she jumped out to greet me. She seemed so pleased to see me and I apologised for ever doubting that she would be a star. I don't think she heard me – she was just being Katie for a minute and was very nervous about her first reporting job.

When I recently watched the fly-on-the-wall reality TV show *Katie* (previously *What Katie Did Next*), she seemed so sad and alone. I do hope that, deep inside, there's still a bit of Katie left, and that Jordan has not entirely taken over.

2

The First Cut

Hairdressing was not my first choice of profession; the glittering lights of show business beckoned and what I really wanted to be was an actor. I won a place at the National Youth Theatre – the only kid in my school to get in – though my audition piece, the Quentin Crisp monologue from *The Naked Civil Servant,* did raise a few eyebrows. I also managed to get onto an art course at Newcastle Art and Design after I finished my O levels.

My first experience of hairdressing was the Hollywood version – Warren Beatty's *Shampoo.* The X-rated film was for over-18s only and I was just 14. But that didn't deter my inventive father, who really wanted to see the film: he stuck a cigarette in my mouth and told me to keep quiet as he bought the tickets. It worked and we were able to sneak in.

Dad loved the film – he fancied himself as Warren Beatty, sleeping with all the clients and generally behaving badly. I loved it too, but for a different reason – that trip to the cinema was one of the few times I can remember that Dad and I actually got on. He still likes talking about films and it's one of the few things that we have in common.

Nothing I did was ever good enough for my dad, and I failed at anything he ever tried to teach me. He spent hours showing me how to tie my shoelaces, shouting at me because I couldn't manage it. To this day, I still get in a muddle tying my laces.

He and Mum married young – very young if you listen to Mum. As I shot up in size, she would get me to pretend to be her brother when we went out and about. My parents did their best to bring up my sister Karen and me but they never really had the chance to explore life themselves. Dad, who was a director at British Gas, played the trumpet and wanted to be a jazz musician. He had a strained relationship with his own father and that carried on over into the next generation and his relationship with me.

I've almost lost count of the number of times we moved when we were kids. I was born in Coatbridge, Scotland, the place Frankie Boyle said the Ethiopians held a charity concert for. We moved to Livingston when I was eight and then to Whitley Bay. Some months after that rare, happy afternoon at the movies with my father, we moved to Hemel Hempstead, which meant yet another new school for Karen and me. I actually quite liked the new school, and the fact that I was in the National Youth Theatre made me a hit with the excellent theatre group they had there. So I fitted in pretty well, unlike the high school at Whitley Bay, where I had suffered from constant bullying.

But just as things were going well, my parents had one of their almighty rows and, before we knew it, Mum, Karen and I ended up with nowhere to go on a snowy Saturday night. We had no money and had no option but to go to the police station, where they sent us to spend the night in sheltered accommodation. Our friends from Whitley Bay, Linda and Jim, kindly paid for us to go back up north and gave us a roof over our heads till things could be sorted out.

My parents separated and Karen and I went back to our old school in Whitley Bay. The bullying continued but there was less of it, as my appearance in the local papers for getting into the youth theatre did wonders for my popularity – everyone loves a celebrity, no matter how minor!

All in all, I was pretty happy. Dad visited occasionally, although it almost always ended in a horrific row. Mum, who had been a promotion girl at sales events, got a job at Radio Rentals. Then my parents decided to get back together. Mum had gone on a well-earned break with my sister, leaving me to study for my mock GCSEs.

Mum had always wanted to travel and we went to Spain once on holiday as kids. But when she came back from her trip away with my sister she had run out of money and agreed to get back with Dad. We were all moving back to London. When I say London, what I actually mean is Surbiton, and on top of that, we were half an hour's walk from the station. Mum, though, being a born saleswoman, made it sound idyllic.

Thoughts turned to what I would do after my exams. Dad insisted it would be better to get a trade rather than do something wishy-washy like go to art school. As a trade-off, he said that if I got a trade, then I could go to drama school. If I failed at acting, he said, I would have hairdressing to fall back on. Mum and Dad said they knew an actress who almost died of starvation trying to make it into the theatre; and, as my Dad so supportively put it, 'She was genuinely talented.'

My drama teacher, Michael Wilcox, who wrote the acclaimed play, *Rent*, begged me not to go into hairdressing. I would regret it later in life, he said. But since plumbing or anything butch was going to be a 'no-no' for me, Dad suggested cutting hair.

Hairdressing did interest me, and I was happy that I would be able to go to drama school afterwards. It was good to have Dad's approval too. I think he suggested hairdressing because he pictured himself sleeping with the clients, and that's certainly why a lot of straight men get into the business. They see it as sex on tap and take full advantage. Some just can't keep it in their trousers. One straight guy I used to work with would measure the length of his long-haired clients' by laying it on their breasts – followed by his hand. Many women would just sit there and let him do it. Another would take clients up to the sunroom on the top floor, where they would get rather more than a blow-dry.

It was shortly before we moved to the not-so-bright lights of Surbiton that my parents discovered I was gay. I had just turned 16. My best friend at school, Sally Perkins, became pregnant and, because I was really concerned about her, I told Mum and Dad.

Mum's reaction was instant – she put her hair up. This was always the signal that she was in a really bad mood. Maybe that's why, to this day, I still prefer hair down when styling rather than up. To my utter amazement, she thought I was the father and launched into one of her rants.

Taking absolutely no notice of my protestations of innocence, she took off in the car with my father, wearing her bright red suit – and with a face to match. She was still raging when she returned although my dad seemed smugly satisfied that I had turned out to be a wrong 'un after all.

She would bring up the baby, she declared imperiously. That's all very well, I told her, but I felt she ought to know that the child was most definitely not mine as I was gay and dating Gary, the judo expert. You could have heard a pin drop. At first, Mum thought I was making it up to stop her getting back with my father. 'I preferred the baby story,' she finally squealed.

I know it's always a shock for a parent to find out that their child is gay. I have done hair for clients whose sons are practically in drag but they still seem so surprised when they turn out not to be straight. Funnily enough, my dad reacted pretty sympathetically; I think he was relieved in a way and took it to be the reason why he and I had never really connected. It was also one up on Mum. She became a nightmare over the whole thing, which she found very hard to handle. Having raised me to be independent, she now started to try to control me, as though that would suddenly make me turn straight.

16

My darling sister, who was only 13 at the time, asked me what tragedy it was that had sent Mum into such a spin. 'You're gay, right?' She already knew, she said, and gave me a lovely little kiss. I always felt sorry for my sister, who is a Pisces, living with three Geminis. She is still my best friend to this day, although she's my very worst client. I have tried paying her to go elsewhere but she hates anyone else doing her hair despite moaning constantly whenever I set to work on her thick locks. She sent me a video of a haircut she'd had done recently over in the States and was not happy with, asking me what she should do with it. I called it 'The Ring 3' – anyone who sees it dies within seven days!

So, some months later I found myself living in Surbiton. Karen had a new school, Tolworth Girls' School, where she made new friends but I knew no one. Worse still, I was miles away from London, from any theatre groups or any of my kind of people.

I hoped I would make friends when I found my first job as a hairdressing apprentice at Dickins & Jones in Richmond. It took 45 minutes to get there each day and I earned £16 a week, of which I had to give £4 to Mum for housekeeping. The other problem was that I had to be in by eleven o'clock every night, as Mum seemed to think that, being gay, things happened late at night that could not happen during the day.

I was truly miserable. From being allowed to look after myself when she went away on holiday and frequently looking after my sister, I was now hardly trusted to do anything and there were so many new rules.

During my first time out in London, I popped into a gay bar at lunchtime and started to make friends. A young air steward invited me to a party the following Sunday and said that a car would be sent for me. He would not tell me whose home it was, but said it would be great fun.

I slipped out on the Sunday and picked up the car at the end of the road, where the steward was waiting with the driver. As we reached the destination, I was stunned by what I saw – it was the most magnificent house, more of a mansion really, with statues of a butler and maids to greet you in the huge entrance hall. It was like nothing I had ever seen before.

We parked the car at the back of the house and went to meet our host at the tennis court. I was shocked when I saw who he was – he had played with one of my favourite bands when I was growing up and here he was greeting me on his tennis court! He was down to earth and seemed genuinely interested in me. Before long we ended up in his disco, where the cocktails flowed. And that's not all: some of the other guests offered me cocaine and laughed when I refused. 'Hey, have you brought a good kid to the party?' they said. Still, it was a great day, and I went home with my host's autograph. That was enough excitement for me. As he brought me home the steward suggested I might like to meet other friends of his and intimated that it could be quite profitable for me. But I was streetwise beyond my 16 years, and said no thanks.

So I was somewhat surprised when I received a call from the star's right-hand man asking me to come down again, which I did. I found myself liking the guy, who even played a song for me, but really I preferred T. Rex. He only stopped sending for me after I told him that I'd mentioned the visits to my family. He almost passed out! After all, I was still only 16. All these years later, though, whenever I smell Opium perfume, I think of him. The fragrance filled the bathrooms in his fabulous house and I even bought some for my mother that Christmas.

I worked like a slave at Dickins & Jones. The cheap detergent shampoo they used was so harsh that as I sat on the bus home blood would drip down the cracks of my hands. The more I tried to moisturise and protect them, the worse they got. Kay, a hairdresser who also worked there, told me to leave my hands and put nothing on them. They got so sore I nearly gave up hairdressing but, after about a month, my hands cleared up as if by magic.

The manager, Robert, kept promising proper training but I could count the training nights on the fingers of one hand. When Robert left he was replaced by a very charismatic stylist called Andre, who promised lots of training and created an exciting atmosphere in the salon. But there was more trouble with my hands as I suffered a horrible outbreak of warts, probably because of the water. It took a month of agonising treatment to get rid of them.

When I returned, I was made Andre's personal junior. He had some great clients such as Lynne Frederick, Peter Sellers' actress wife, and her mother Iris, who very sweetly gave me tickets to take my mum to watch a recording of *Man About the House*. Andre also did the hair of the ultra glamorous model and Hammer Horror actress Madeline Smith, who was even prettier in real life than she was on the screen. It was a treat to wash her hair. The formal training promised by Andre had not materialised but I was picking up lots of tips from him.

Things were going well when, almost overnight, I was demoted from manager's junior to general junior. Andre replaced me with a pretty girl who apparently had more experience, though I later discovered that her experience lay in areas other than blow-drying.

Having not had a single class in six months I handed in my notice and went to work for a shop up the road, run by Neville and David who used to work in the West End. They rushed you through your apprenticeship and had you working on the floor quicker than most shops, which meant more money. And after the summer I would go to college.

There was only one small problem – my mind works a bit like a dodgy computer, which means that, although I digest information, it does not drop into my e-mail inbox till a few days later. Once it has arrived, I'm usually better than most people at acting upon it, but in this formative period, this delay in processing what I was learning meant that I was hopeless at hairdressing to start out with and got into a right state trying to do the simplest of tasks.

One particular day, when Neville's patience with me was getting a bit strained anyway, he asked me to take some foil highlights out for one of his favourite clients. Feeling a little nervous, I busied myself removing each foil, talking too much to cover the nerves. Suddenly I looked in the mirror, and the untinted bits of the hair had turned bright orange. Naturally enough, the client screamed. Neville almost fainted, but he got himself together enough to fire me on the spot. 'Hairdressing just ain't for you, love,' were his parting words.

That should have been the end of my hairdressing career, but as I sniffled my way home I remembered my pottery teacher, Mrs Wilkson. She had been my favourite teacher at Whitley Bay and had told me I would always start out slow but that with praise and encouragement I would be the best in the class. I just knew that I could still be an amazing hairdresser.

So within a week I was working at Charles of Wimbledon. He and his mother had two shops and although they did not send me to college they did give classes and sent me to Jingles Hairdressing Academy after six months. I started to pick up quickly there and was blow-drying clients within a few months. I was also allowed to apply tints to clients and that meant more tips.

One particularly busy day I had all the clients' colour cards out in the stock room and picked up the last one of the day. I mixed up the hair colour with the peroxide and applied it to the client's hair. A few minutes later, when the stylist asked where her client's card was, I told her I had put it away as I had applied the tint. Her face fell, as she had not put the card out and I had applied the wrong colour; her client was now rapidly turning brown instead of blonde. Naturally, I was entirely to blame; there was no thought that maybe a 16-year-old who had not even taken a colour course should not be doing ten tints in a day, not to mention shampooing, cleaning and missing lunch.

Despite this, and even though they did not really like my flamboyant behaviour, my enthusiasm and hard work paid off and I was sent to Jingles Academy. The teachers were fabulously trendy and it was like being at theatre school except we were cutting hair. Well, I would have been cutting hair if I could have stopped my hands shaking for long enough to cut a straight line. My nerves had got to me – one chap leapt out of the chair as I almost cut his ear off. On reflection, though, you couldn't blame him.

Years later, when I was opening the hairdressing section of Hertford Regional College, I was introduced as 'the GMTV celebrity hairdresser' and asked to talk about qualifications, and in particular NVQ exams. My heart sank – I wasn't sure what they were. I had passed exams to work as a hairdresser in California, where I lived for eight years, but it wasn't necessary to have qualifications to work in the UK back then.

As I went to speak in front of the teachers and all the students I froze for a second, not sure what to say. But then I remembered what a good teacher can bring – inspiration and confidence, turning raw students into top stylists. A bad teacher will do the opposite. So I just muttered something about the exams and made my talk about just that – teaching.

I do think some apprenticeships are just cheap labour. If the salon you are training in is not sending you to college and allowing you to do at least two model nights a week right from day one then you should find a new salon. (Model night are the evenings held for the training juniors, when members of the public plus friends and family can come in and get styled at a discount.)

Places such as Sassoon are great for apprentices, as long as you do not think for one second that you are going on the cruise liners when you finish. Some of the kids coming out of there cannot hold a round brush, let alone put hair up for a glamorous ball, but they can cut and colour, depending upon their chosen specialism. Expect to spend another year in an industrial salon, if you go down the Sassoon route, before working in a hotel or travelling abroad. However, the kudos of being Sassoon trained sets you up for life, as it is recognised and respected around the world.

By the time I got back to the salon, after my Jingles training, my nerves had settled and I was a good little basic haircutter. As well as cutting I was colouring – all at junior wages, of course. But tips were good and at least I did not have to clean the mirrors with methylated spirits all day and pass up rollers to the stylists.

One day there was a huge snowstorm which made it impossible for me to get to Wimbledon by public transport. So I walked there from Surbiton and arrived two hours late and extremely cold. Only a skeleton staff had made it in at all and Mr Charles seemed amazed that I had managed it. That did not stop him declaring that he was docking half a day's wages because I was late. With that, he put on his coat and left.

After that I was determined not to waste any more time there, but then I wasn't crazy about cleaning floors again. So I applied to work as a stylist for the trendy Ginger Group in Kingston where, luckily, the manager liked my style. I had to pass a test and, even luckier for me, the two cuts I was required to do were the ones I had learnt at Jingles. When I handed in my notice to Mr Charles he muttered something about suing me for the Jingles course and how he had never liked me.

On the subject of never liking me, much as Clive at the Ginger Group seemed happy to see me on my first day, the rest of the staff could barely say hello. It seemed I had replaced one of their chums who got sent off to another salon. It became their sole purpose to get me to leave. Having put up with years of relentless bullying at school, though, I took their hostility in my stride. In fact, it was all going well until my three haircuts dried up and clients started to complain. To be honest, I'd have got away with it if it hadn't been for the fact that one of the hairdressers from Wimbledon, who knew I was working there, told the manager I was only 17. In fact I was still only 16.

Rather than fire me, Clive got me a job in the Ealing branch as a junior stylist, which meant I was still taking classes but got to do clients too. I loved it there, it was so trendy and there were other gay people working there, though the manager, Steve, made it clear he was not overly keen on camp behaviour.

Pretty soon I was earning enough to leave home and moved to my first flat in Chiswick, above a jewellers. It had a shower in the bedroom that used to leak all the time but I loved it and it gave me the freedom to be myself and have a real social life for the first time.

But I fell in love with Brighton after a sunny weekend there and decided I wanted to live by the sea. I applied for a job at a new salon, Crown's, run by a small energetic man called Peter Crown. He had a sister shop in Worthing and was one of the first to sell products from Body Shop, which was based in nearby Littlehampton.

One of my clients was Anita Roddick, the founder of The Body Shop, though she was reluctant when she first came into the salon, complaining to the receptionist that all the hairdressers Peter had hired were too young. Her face fell when I asked how she would like her hair. Back then she had it blow-dried straight, which was my speciality. Halfway through the blow-dry she put her hands through her hair to check how it was doing. 'You are really good,' she said, with surprise. She was a lovely woman and her ideas were truly unique.

Peter Crown thought I was great and perfect for the Brighton salon; he gave me such confidence in my work and really pushed me. However, Mr Crown really liked his pound of flesh – if you were not cutting hair, he wanted you cleaning or doing something else and the pay was very poor. He was clever though, in realising that opening super-glamorous salons and filling them with predominantly young, trendy and exciting staff brought in the clients. He also knew that he could get away with paying us less than the older staff. He encouraged us to get mortgages at a young age, partly to teach us good money management but also, I think, to tie us to the security of working for him.

I was fully booked almost from the start, as the colourful Brighton clientele of theatrical types and antique dealers took a shine to me. I hit lucky as my very first client there was a popular socialite, who told everyone about me; next was Susan Maughan, a truly stunning 1960s beauty who had, most famously, sung *Bobby's Girl*. I was terrified of doing her the first time but I loved her hair. She was a true lady and sent clients to me. Almost 30 years later, my friend Lester Middlehurst interviewed her and mentioned me when she was performing at the Café Royal in Regent Street; she rang and invited me along.

But much as being a colourful character went down well with the clients, it did not brush well with the staff. I got on well with Jane Shepard and Chris Eubank's wife Karen, but generally I was not well liked. Peter constantly tried to get me to conform and to work quietly, and to do cleaning in between clients.

That was never going to happen, so in the end I handed in my notice. Peter was speechless and ran after me demanding to know why I was leaving. He blamed everyone and everything apart from his dictatorial style of management. But I truly thank him for the confidence he gave me.

With that, I walked through the Brighton Lanes and at 18 became a self-employed stylist at a wonderful salon called Harleys. It meant no cleaning up and no rules. My life was really about to change for the better.

3

A Gay Man Trapped in a Woman's Body

'I am a gay man trapped in a woman's body…'
Madonna

I was at the showbiz restaurant, The Ivy, with my best friend of over 30 years, the actress and presenter Denise Welch, and other pals. We were sipping champagne and gossiping when Denise suddenly blurted out: 'I'm just a gay man trapped in a woman's body!' We all burst out laughing, and laughed even more as one friend swiftly retorted: 'No, love, you're just a gay man.'

He had a point – with her camp, outrageous behaviour, Denise could start a party in an empty room, even though she has battled against depression for years. And she'd flirt with a lamppost if no one else was around! If she had been born a man, she would definitely be gay.

The next time we met up was a sadder occasion. Our mutual friend, the Machiavellian, outrageous, talented *Daily Mail* journalist Lester Middlehurst had apparently taken his own life, after fighting depression and addiction problems in recent years. He was only 55 and we had known him for almost three decades. He could be antagonistic but Denise and I loved him dearly and he was a true friend.

I first set eyes on Denise at Lester's home in Kemp Town, Brighton, which he shared with his lover Paul Cooper. Denise attended drama school with his red-headed cousin, Rosemary

Hirst. My first thought, as she sat sipping coffee and giggling with Rosemary, was how stunning Denise was. Lester, though, had nicknamed her the 'Borneo native' as he apparently thought she looked like one without her make-up on. Although he later denied it, Lester was not keen on Denise and only put up with her for Rosemary's sake. Denise was appearing in the Patrick Hamilton play, *Gaslight,* at the Nightingale Theatre, playing the lead, Bella Manningham (made famous by Ingrid Bergman in the 1944 film adaptation); Rose was playing the maid, Nancy.

My friendship with Lester was not instant – on our first meeting he made it clear I was too 'out there' and I guess I took some of the limelight away from him. Our next liaison, at a fancy-dress party, didn't endear me to him – I was on roller-skates dressed as the Martini Boy, which rather upstaged his New Romantic look, and his face fell when he saw me. Much as I tried to win him over, telling him he looked pretty with make-up on, he turned his head, took a drag on his Belair menthol cigarette, and reluctantly murmured, 'Thank you', turning to talk to anyone else he could find.

In the end, whenever we were in the same room, we both resented the other being there. However, journalists love free-bies and I realised there was a way to win him over. Mike Moore, owner of the salon, Harleys, where I worked, had installed the latest and most expensive sunbed in Brighton, and Lester loved to tan. Knowing that publicity, especially free publicity, would be good for the salon, I came up with the idea of having an ex-beauty queen have Harleys 'tattooed' on her stomach, by placing the words in a stencil on her tummy and then putting her on the bed. When we took the stencil off, the white words stood out against her newly brown skin. I pitched the idea to Lester as an *Evening Argus* story, promising him a free course of sunbed treatment, of course, and it made a page in the paper. Lester was happily brown.

It was not long before Mr Middlehurst was in my chair having burgundy lowlights, though he said, as he sat down, 'My old hairdresser says they are called red streaks and they are half the price where she works.'

Despite our initial differences we became inseparable, though volatile, friends.

Meanwhile, Denise had fallen in love with Brighton and came back to look for a property there. Her then husband, David Easter, whom she'd met whilst starring in the stage version of *Grease*, was due to join her later. When the gorgeous David eventually arrived, he was a real treat to the eyes. As soon as Lester saw the hunk, Denise became his new best friend; as far as Lester was concerned, the 'Borneo native' could stay as long as she liked – as long as her husband walked around in his underpants.

Heads certainly turned in Brighton when Mr Easter walked down the street, even when he wasn't in his underpants! Denise and he became the golden couple and seemed so in love. Denise and Rose were like sisters and were regulars in my salon chair, and David also became a client and good friend. In fact, it was one of the happiest times of my life; it was like one big happy family. Even my sister Karen had moved out of home and had come to live in Brighton with me.

But things started to change once David and Denise got their first flat in Kemp Town. David would often protest about people looking at him and gay men making passes at him, though he always claimed he didn't mind gay men fancying him. Neither Lester nor I could figure out who these people were, as he was always with our gang and neither of us had made a move on him, even though Lester was notorious at straight baiting (trying to turn straight men gay) and would boast of his conquests to me and anyone who would listen.

Friday night was notorious as gay night at Waitrose in Brighton yet David would insist on shopping there in a tight string vest and clinging leather shorts, which left nothing to the imagination. Every time someone looked at him, he would shrug his shoulders, and say: 'I can't believe it keeps happening.' He became almost paranoid when he got into the now defunct soap, *Brookside*, playing the part of Pat Hancock. We gave him a first episode party at Lester's and he suddenly seemed to change. Though he was only in the soap for a minute, with a bit part driving a van, he acted as though he was the next Marlon Brando And he became critical of Denise – if she had one cigarette, for example, he would accuse her of being out of control.

David and I would regularly meet for lunch or a drink when he was down in Brighton and we were due to get together a few weeks after his debut on *Brookside*. On the day, he called to say he did not want to meet at our usual pub as there might be too many fans there. To be honest, it was hard not to laugh; he had initially only had a tiny part in *Brookside* and anyway Brighton is a celebrity stomping ground, so locals pay little attention to real stars, let alone two-bit soap actors. To humour him, we went to a new bar but he could not concentrate on the conversation and we had to move chairs twice in case people recognised him. As I headed back to work, I had a bad feeling about David and worried for Denise.

I learned early on that the messenger always gets shot when giving unwelcome news about someone's partner, and that is an important thing to remember when doing hair. When I teach juniors how to handle clients, I tell them to keep to the subject – their client's hair – and not to ask about husbands or boyfriends unless the client brings it up. At all costs, do not give opinions, unless it's on what restaurant, movie or plastic surgeon to go to, and most top hairdressers will know the answers to all of the above. It is wise to stay out of your clients' personal lives, as it will only come back and bite you!

Strangely, that afternoon, an attractive and smartly dressed woman we will call Mrs S came into the salon and asked for me to blow-dry her hair. I had a space, so had her washed and started to blow-dry, enquiring whether I had been recommended to her. She quietly replied, no. Once I finished, she booked to come in two days later for a perm.

On the day she was due I heard a car drive at speed up the small road by the shop. It came to a screeching stop and a woman was pushed out of the door, followed by her handbag, the contents of which scattered across the road. The car sped off, leaving the woman – my client, Mrs S – sprawled on the pavement.

We rushed out of the salon but she refused help. She swiftly regained her dignity and walked into the salon as if nothing had happened. She said very little and simply went upstairs for a sunbed treatment.

When she came to have her hair done, she said very little again and when I asked whether she was OK, she just nodded. It was as I was finishing her hair that she murmured that her male partner hit her and that she had some problems. I said I was sorry to hear that and that she should not let it happen. I asked whether she was OK to go home. Mrs S looked down at the floor then up at me, nodded and smiled.

The following Saturday she came in for a day of beauty treatment, including highlights. She had been at the salon for quite a while and asked me to call her partner to explain that she was still there, having her hair done. It seems he was suspicious that she was having an affair. As I picked up the phone, I knew I was making a mistake getting involved and, sure enough, I was met with a barrage of abuse. 'You fucking queer, you're fucking my Mrs.' The statement did not make sense, which I pointed out; if I was queer, then how could I be messing around with his wife? 'Have a nice day,' I told him and hung up. Before I did, he threatened to come down to the shop and kill me, so I double locked the door just in case!

The next week Mrs S booked her husband in for a haircut. I was speechless at first – what was she thinking? But he had calmed down by then and in fact, though he was rough around the edges, he could not have been nicer, although he was the complete opposite of his elegant wife. I had dinner with them several times and became extremely fond of Mrs S, and she became a great friend. But I saw that she would deliberately provoke him and it was clear she got a kick out of it. It was a very dysfunctional relationship and they were playing games with each other. By getting involved with Mrs S I had become an unwilling pawn in their game. She would tell him that she fancied me more than him, just to provoke a reaction. They say being a hairdresser you sometimes become a therapist, but it pays to remember that good therapists let the client make their own decisions and rarely give their own opinions.

One great thing came of our friendship: Mrs S introduced me to her bridge-playing friend, Martin Annand. Though Martin was not enamoured of me on our first meeting, months later an 18-year relationship began.

Martin soon became friends with my group of pals, although, predictably, Lester was not as welcoming. He found Martin a threat for my attention. As Martin came from a public school background, and I most certainly did not, Lester would call me Eliza Doolittle behind my back, knowing full well that the gossipy queens who frequented the Lanes' shops would be sure to pass it on. But in the end we all became friends and Martin and I even went on holiday together with Lester and his long-term partner.

With the amount of publicity I was receiving in the *Evening Argus*, thanks to Lester and his room-mate, Helen Galley, who also worked as a journalist on the paper, my client list was getting longer. But along with that came the difficult clients who expect you to work magic. If you look a little deeper you can usually work out why they are like that. Sometimes it's a psychological problem, such as body dysmorphic disorder (BDD), which is when people have a crippling and often distorted self-image. Often, it goes back to childhood: recently a client who could not have her hair 'big enough' confided that her mother had always told her as a little girl that she had thin hair. So that presumably explains why she always wanted bigger hair. When you find out what the problem is, it makes it easier to take care of the client's needs.

One of my clients was the top soap celebrity Amanda Barrie, of *Coronation Street*, and she would often wear wigs on and off set despite having the thickest and most beautiful hair. I used to call them her Yorkshire terriers. When I started to do her hair, she reeled off the list of dreadful hairdressers she had been to, many big names among them. When she got to Vidal Sassoon, she stopped: 'He once did make me a great hair piece,' she said. Sure enough she smiled when I finished and said her hair was lovely, but went on to tell her girlfriend (also a friend of mine) how awful it was. I knew when she got to Vidal himself there was no chance of pleasing her.

Despite this, she came back a month later, staying with me for almost two years. We only fell out when she started to instruct me on how to cut her girlfriend's bob haircut. 'Point cut it!' she commanded, telling me it made the bob thicker as she tried to grab the scissors from my hand. Of course, it does the oppo-site. Standing up to her did not go down well.

There was a woman called Jane who was so neurotic about her bleached hair that most hairdressers in Brighton dreaded her appearing in their chair. Sure enough, after seeing a blonde friend of hers who worked in a local sandwich shop, my turn came. To my surprise, she was happy once the final touches had been done. On the way out she told me: 'The only nice thing my mum ever said to me was you look nice blonde.' That explained why she was so neurotic about her hair colour and why it was so important to her, and it made it much easier to look after her.

Her joy did not last long when she became obsessed about perming her hair. I told her point blank that it was too coloured to take a perm and she nagged and nagged, questioning my ability to perm. As fate would have it, we were asked to find a client to demonstrate a new computer perm the salon was being sent from London with a top technician. Being a little naughty, I suggested Jane as the client, knowing full well that the technician would reel in horror at her over-processed hair and that would put an end to her nagging. To my surprise, the technician agreed to perform the perm.

Jane was full of herself as she basked in how wrong my professional opinion had been. The perm was attached to the computer and it had only been processing for two minutes when an alarm buzzed. 'Ready,' said the technician, though he looked rather worried. He neutralised her at the wash-basin and wrapped her hair in a towel and handed her over to me, while he quickly packed up and left. Her hair was completely frazzled. Of course, she blamed me and made my life hell. In fact she was at the front door when we opened the next day. We had to get the company who made the perm to look after her at home and they had to pay her compensation. That was the worst hair experience I had ever had, and it was not even of my making.

Harleys was the nicest shop to work in. My friends would drop in and it was a real family atmosphere. Denise was starting to make waves in the show business world and was away doing a play, leaving her husband David alone.

Inevitably there was trouble ahead. One Saturday morning I took a call from a client, Suzy, assuming she wanted to book an appointment. But she had something else on her mind.

'Hi, Steve, listen, I was with David Easter last night and he left without giving me his number. Can you give it to me?' My first thought was that she had met him at a club with friends, but my mouth dropped open when it dawned on me what she really meant. Quickly I pointed out that he was married to my best friend, but she was having none of that, so to get her off the phone I took her number and promised to pass it on to David.

The next surprise was that Mandy, one of the junior stylists, seemed to know something about it, as she had been at the Kings Club where David and Suzy spent the evening and saw them leave together. If there is a downside to living in Brighton – or London by the Sea, as it's known – it's that everyone knows your business, especially among the Lanes' community.

I rang David, who sounded groggy, and told him about the phone call. He protested his innocence and said he had been out for a few drinks and Suzy had hassled him. He asked me not to give her his number or to mention it to Denise who was away for the week. Naively, I bought it.

But there were other sightings of him and Suzy and rumours began to emerge of him having a thing with one of the Harleys staff.

Denise was always an incredibly sexual creature – that was what we initially had in common. Our birthdays fall within days of each other, so we are both Gemini and very similar to one another. I think the main attraction with David was his great staying power in the bedroom, something she always said was the most important thing in a man to her. I remember one evening when she was staying at Lester's, sharing the front room fold-down bed with cousin Rose. I was having a dalliance with a bit of a hunk and, unable to contain themselves, they crawled on all fours to the landing to watch. They could not stop giggling the next morning and gave me votes! I was shocked to start with but we still laugh about it now.

But she was really trying to be a good wife to David, who

went on about fidelity and would give her a hard time if she even looked at another guy. Denise always says to me, 'If Jesus had known we were going to live so long, he would've given us a couple of choices,' but, being young, she gave it her all in her relationship with David. In my opinion he was clearly an egotist and his main love was himself.

It was not long before Denise got wind of David's infidelities and they separated. It's impossible to keep secrets in Brighton, and of course Lester heard and could not wait to tell. To cheer Denise up, Martin and I took her skiing to the Royals' favourite resort, Klosters in Switzerland. Martin is an extremely dashing man and with Denise being a stunner, everyone thought they were the ideal couple. Denise just wanted the *aprés-ski*, but Martin offered to get us our own ski instructor in the form of a six-foot hunk, Florien. Martin, being an advanced skier, had a different instructor, and noted that Florien was very popular with the girls.

Over lunch, while Denise was in the ladies, I told Florien that Denise was an actress and a Bond girl, which really got his attention. I let Denise in on the white lie and she played along and soon had the stud eating out of her hand. Denise has something: no matter how many beautiful women are in the room she can get any man she chooses; she is just a man-magnet. By the end of the trip she was spending nights in Florien's quarters, enjoying his amazing staying power. She shared the details with me on the flight home!

Denise went on to have a few dalliances with men, most of whom I liked, and even one with Robert Rawles who played the milkman in *Keeping up Appearances*. He would drive me up the wall whenever he appeared; there was just something about him that wound me up. Denise would get cross with me when I asked her what she saw in him; it was good that it did not last long.

Martin was the senior finance director at a branch of an American company, Born Heaters. The owner's wealthy bachelor son, Sidney Born, who was also the vice president of the company, was in town and the directors were taking turns entertaining him. I had met him briefly and thought that another boring dinner at home or at a stuffy restaurant did not look like his cup of tea, so when it came to Martin's turn I suggested a people carrier of eight lovely girls and a night out at Stringfellows.

I was right – the handsome Yank thought he'd died and gone to heaven! Denise was among the bevy of lovelies that night and her younger sister Debbie came down from Newcastle. Sidney had spent the night chatting to Debbie and it seemed there was a great connection. Denise got plastered with me and though she was nice to Sidney there was no real chemistry.

We nicknamed him Sid the Limp because he had been left with a limp after childhood polio. The next day he left Martin in no doubt that not only had it been the best evening of his life but he was also very taken with Denise and wanted her number. Denise was a little taken aback when he called, but agreed to go to dinner with him to help Martin's business. He picked her up in a Rolls-Royce, with two Kir Royales ready. Despite being American, Sid the Limp had a great sense of humour and understood irony and it was not long before Denise was on the phone telling me she was smitten.

The other directors were a little put out as the only place Sidney wanted to be was with Denise or us. He was handsome and had a great Southern drawl, and during a passionate evening with Denise he promised to fly her to Venice and make love to her there.

A week or so later it was my birthday and Martin promised to take me to the famous Joe Allen Restaurant in London. He decided to drive there as he had a package that needed dropping off at Gatwick to be sent by private plane. I was looking forward to the evening and waited in the car as Martin took the small package into the Portakabin at the airport. After a few minutes he came out and told me there was a problem and said I would have to come in and wait for a bit. As I walked in, I saw Denise and Sidney, then Lester and Paul and my mother!

Joe Allen was cancelled as dinner was booked in Paris and the planes were on stand-by to take us there. Arriving in Paris, we went by limo to Le Grand Véfour restaurant in the Rue Du Beaujolais and had the most wonderful dinner. There was another lovely surprise in that my wonderful friend Bill Jeavons had been driven from Brighton by car for the evening. As he was suffering from cancer, he was too poorly to travel by plane. The evening was a dream come true and after dinner we all drove to the Sacré Cœur and took in the sights. Denise turned to Sidney, asking: 'Does this mean we're not going to Venice?' It meant no such thing. As the rest of us took off to fly home, Denise and Sidney flew to Venice for a romantic weekend. This was 1986 and it was a birthday neither Denise nor I will ever forget.

Denise's torrid affair with Sidney continued. There was talk of her moving to Tulsa, Oklahoma, and the thought of her living there had us all in tears. The vision of Denise in the religious South, raising perfect children, just didn't seem to fit. Sidney even offered to buy her a little rep company. Denise's mum, Annie, was very excited about her daughter becoming a millionaire's wife, and had a vision of living a life like in *Dallas*, the popular TV show of the time. But Denise was never going to be a Sue Ellen. Martin and I tried to convince her that she would hate Oklahoma, playing the perfect Southern wife. Poor Denise can't cook to save her life; she once made me a roast chicken and sat and watched me eat every mouthful. This was a rare event. 'You're brave,' her son Matthew said, as he looked on.

Weeks later Denise discovered that Sidney's staying power had more than proved itself; she was pregnant. She rang to tell him from a telephone box but it was clear he did not want to know;

he offered to send her whatever money she needed. The pregnancy was terminated. She was incredibly brave and as always picked herself up and went on with life. Denise has the ability to appear fine when inside she is dying and it's only when you get to know her well that you can see that even though she's laughing, she's in pain.

Sidney's father had pulled him back to the States and managed to convince his son that it was a youthful dalliance and he was best giving up the Brit actress. In the end Denise agreed it was for the best, though we had to break the news to Annie carefully, as she was still dreaming of having a millionaire son-in-law.

It is easy to see why Denise is how she is – her mum is a real glamour puss and has a great sense of humour. Denise's dad, Vin, is also quite a character – he has an alter ego called Raquel, and he loves to dress up in character. We took him to a transsexual restaurant in Earls Court one evening and he looked amazing. Vin can party all night and into the next day and I think he would like to have been Denise.

Life was changing for all of us. Lester had started going up to London to do shift work at the *Mail* and *Express* in the hope of getting a staff job, though being almost a junior there he was given the jobs the others did not want, such as ringing Diana Dors up to get a quote about her cancer coming back. He once rang me from a bar in the East End of London where he was sent to track down one of the Price sisters, who had been jailed for their part in the IRA car bombs in London in 1973. He was so nervous he even asked me to go along. But I had two clients waiting, and I had little doubt that, if he did find her, she'd soon be his new best friend.

Lester eventually went to work at *Today* newspaper, where of course he was everyone's darling. At the same time, the naughty schoolboy drove everyone mad with his gossiping and need for love and approval. He developed a long-term friendship with the columnist and writer Jane Moore at *Today*, though she was wise to him early on and kept any love interest a secret. Jane had been dating the handsome James Sheldon, who worked on the picture desk, for a full six months before Lester found out. Lester was speechless, not just because he fancied James himself, but because he had not been able to interfere for six months. This is James, who later went on to have a beautiful daughter, Ellie, with Jane! We always laugh about the story.

Lester broke up with his long-term partner, Paul, and started a relationship with the actor Dean Sullivan, whom he'd met whilst covering a murder mystery weekend. Whilst slipping off to a private room, the two got down to bare facts only to be interrupted by two budding lady sleuths. At first Lester and Dean were red faced, but the Miss Marples thought it was part of the plot and took notes and left! Dean went on to star as Jimmy Corkhill in Channel 4's *Brookside* and he and Lester bought a small terraced house in South East London. But the relationship was turbulent and only lasted a few years.

I started doing some magazine work, kicking off with doing the hair for the covers for celebrity clairvoyant Eva Petulengro's monthly astrology magazine, and I was getting a taste for session work.

On a holiday in California, Martin and I were looking at the Golden Gate Bridge, when he asked, 'Shall we move here?' As we drove down Route 101 towards Los Angeles, getting as far as Clint Eastwood's town, Carmel, we both knew that we wanted to live in America. If there was any doubt in my mind, on our first night out in Los Angeles we were dining at the celebrity hang-out Nicky Blair's, when I saw one of my childhood idols, Lucille Ball, at the next table! When 'Lucy' got up she smiled at me and I just blurted out, 'You are truly amazing!' My face went as red as her hair and I wondered whether I had done the right thing but to my surprise and delight she stopped and thanked me and had a quick chat, wishing me a great holiday.

After dinner our host, Tony Anderson, whisked me into Beverly Hills to have drinks at the home of the woman he affectionately called 'The Widow Feldman', Lauretta Sullivan, wife of the late actor and comedian Marty Feldman. She had been married to Marty from 1959 until his death of a heart attack in 1982. She was in her nightdress when we arrived but was very pleased to see us, as some guests that had bored her to tears had just left. I worried that I would bore her too but it must have gone OK because when I left she gasped: 'Darling, I have no idea why you are going back to the UK – you are made for here!' Within the next few months, Martin and I made plans to try the American dream.

4

In God We Trust

'In God We Trust...'
US Department of the Treasury

It was the strictly vegetarian birthday party of Chevy Chase, the actor and comedian, and my friend Morag Kerr and I were hiding behind a screen having a crafty cigarette. The scene, in the glittering ballroom of the Beverly Hills Hilton, more or less summed up LA. Morag, who could go through two packs of Players a day, was desperate for a cigarette but, as smoking was banned at the evening event, we needed to hide away from health-conscious eyes.

Morag, caterer to the stars, was from East Kilbride in Scotland and she was a delight. She was a little neurotic and a great laugh, and when she was not catering or looking after celebrities, she was full of gossip. One prospective client called to ask whether she was Jewish. 'By profession of course, dear,' Morag replied, in her best upper-class Scottish accent. It didn't matter that she was far from posh; Americans thought she was the business. Warren Beatty overheard her voice at the *Dick Tracy* party and, clearly thinking she was a guest, started a conversation with her. Before she knew it, she was being introduced to Madonna. They both looked a little shocked when eventually she piped up: 'Well, this is all very nice, but I need to get the canapés out!' and took her leave.

Of course, when I say it summed up LA, it wasn't long before another secret smoker joined us behind the screen, and then another and then another. Before we knew it there were more people hiding behind the screen than it could hold; it must have looked like a Native American tepee from which some young brave was sending up smoke signals! It was a lovely evening, though. Chevy played piano and I learnt that polenta is very dull, no matter what you do with it, nor how many diners pronounce it delicious and declare they will be vegetarians from that evening forth. Of course, in true LA style, they would never follow through – half of them would be at the drive-through McDonald's on the way home.

LA is full of dog walkers who are actresses and waiters who are the next big thing waiting to happen. It has personal trainers who tell you what to eat and what to do, and every other fad in the world seems to start in LaLa land. Groups like AA and NA provide invaluable help for those with genuine problems but in LA there are some who use them as networking opportunities. Looking at the queues to get in at 1am or 2am, you'd think it was the first day of the Harrods sale rather than a self-help meeting for addicts. One meeting on Robinson Boulevard draws more crowds than a first night. I would sit at the Abbey coffee shop on Sundays, watching them all pile out of the meeting. A lot of them would come over for a latte after and it was great listening to them talking about themselves with such intensity. Unlike the British, it's not uncommon to meet up with Americans who will tell you the most graphic details of their lives on the first meeting, leading the unsuspecting Brit to believe they have made a true friend. But it takes just as long to make real friends in the US as it does in the UK and many of those Americans who shared so much initially will barely remember you when you run into them the following day.

There's a plus side to it: in LA they're enthusiastic about all your ideas, even if they're not good ones, just so they can say they told you so if it does turn out to be a winner. It's easy to retrain in something or reinvent yourself in LA. If you change career in the UK at 30 you'll always hear, 'Oh, are you sure?' and, 'Ooh, I don't know, it's a bit risky.' That's certainly not the case in LA.

Americans network like nobody on the planet. At a party, they'll make you feel like the most important person in the room. At the same time they'll be finding out who you are – and whether you're any use to them – before quickly moving on. It's quite a skill and one that should not be underestimated.

We moved to the States in September 1986 and in my first week in LA I learned all about addiction. Morag, whom I had met through mutual friends while on holiday there a few months before, insisted I stay at her apartment in The Valley. This would help me get used to Tinseltown, she said – that, and the fact that she loved the way I had cut her hair during my last trip. On the day of my arrival she was working for the writer Judith Krantz who, despite having been poorly all day, had decided to push ahead with a dinner party. She needed Morag to stay on and cook, leaving me alone on my first evening.

Morag's lovely neighbour, Susie, volunteered to take me out, and in true LA form she bagged a free haircut whilst promising to buy dinner. However, she said we should both go to an Al-Anon meeting first. It sounded like a plan to me, and I didn't want to tell her I had absolutely no idea what Al-Anon was. Susie was great fun and an actress who did not have to wait tables to supplement her lifestyle (that was considered a success in Los Angeles), so the evening was bound to be a blast.

Al-Anon was indeed a sparkling affair. I was shocked at how many stars were there though more surprised that no drink was available. 'Have you suffered too?' Susie enquired, holding my hand tightly. My face dropped when I finally realised that I was at a family and friends meeting of Alcoholics Anonymous.

A huge Hollywood star, who was in the soap opera *Flamingo Road*, was first to share their experience of dealing with an addictive relative. It was really interesting for a first-timer, rather like being at an interactive theatre show. Coming from the UK, I had always thought that an alcoholic was someone who drank from first thing in the morning until last thing at night. If you have two drinks a night or get out of control on occasions you seem to be labelled an alcoholic in the US. This gave me a new insight, although personally I don't believe having two drinks of an evening makes you an alcoholic. Dinner never happened. Susie apologised, explaining that she had found the speakers moving and needed to get home to gather her thoughts.

Morag was seriously pissed off when she heard I'd been taken to an Al-Anon meeting, and made Susie get a takeaway. 'Dear God, between AA Male Bondage Group,' (her name for a male bonding group popular in America) 'and bloody Al-Anon, if you haven't already got a problem they will bloody well find one for you. Stay clear and no going to therapy. They love that here too!' she laughed, pouring me a large vodka and tonic.

It was in Los Angeles that I first came in contact with the 'plastic fantastic' brigade. A close beautician friend of mine was constantly giving herself chemical peels (where layers of skin are removed to give a fresher look) and she muttered something about going to a surgeon to have a stronger one done.

To my horror, she turned up for lunch several days later looking like Leatherface from *The Texas Chainsaw Massacre*. She didn't seem at all bothered as she nibbled on her macrobiotic salad, telling me it had been a great success. 'Wait till next week, I'll look amazing,' she marvelled, as a bit of her skin dropped off into her salad. She picked it up triumphantly and exclaimed: 'See! It's really working.' I almost brought up my turkey burger.

The problem is that no matter how much surgery you have done, your body ages and unless you are Madonna and can do

Pilates, yoga and exercise obsessively, then your spine will start to bend as you get older.

Look face-on at some of these women and they can look great; with others, though, turn them sideways and it's not so pretty. They may have the face of a 30-year-old but there's no mistaking the dowager hump. It's a scary look, rather like a wicked queen in a fairy-tale who has stolen the face of a beautiful young serving girl.

I am not against a little surgery to freshen the face; it's a bit like keeping your home fresh and up to date – and, let's face it, more people look at your face every day than see your living room.

Botox can often do the trick, but once people are on their third face-lift, scars can clearly be seen beneath their hair or behind the ears. Top surgeons always recommend that you let your hairdressers into your little secret, so they can style accordingly. I knew one hairdresser who was washing his client's hair and kept rubbing behind her ears at what he thought was a black tint mark. The client squealed in horror as her surgery stitches came undone. Quite why he hadn't noticed while applying the tint – or why she had come to the hairdressers at all before having her stitches taken out, or at least told him about it – is beyond me. It is advisable to leave at least a month after the procedure, or until the scars have healed properly, before having your hair coloured.

In youth-obsessed cultures, particularly in the States, clients often lie about having had work done, perhaps trying to fool themselves. One client of mine returned from what she said was a long holiday looking ten years younger; though it was only her face. She was in her late sixties and had a limp from an accident, so her overall look was that of her real age. She came out with the most outlandish explanation for the tell-tale scars in her hair – that she'd had a brain operation! There were scars around her whole hairline and around her ears too. I just smiled and said I'd be careful. What I really wanted to say was, 'Oh really…did the surgeon pull your face up into your brain at the same time?'

By the time a woman has had breast enlargement, face-lifts, lipo, extensions, and wears coloured contacts, as many of the stars do, then just what is left of the real woman? Trust me, a woman who has had nothing done is far sexier than a woman who has tried to turn herself into Pamela Anderson. A strong, confident woman really doesn't need all those things. Those who go too far down the 'plastic fantastic' road are really just trying to mask their insecurities.

After a bit I moved into a small hotel in Santa Monica. I remember my first morning, looking out of my window at the famous pier, which was just like it was in the movies. Glamorous women and men jogged along the sidewalk. But wandering down there later, I saw the other side of the American dream: they were jogging past – or literally over – some of the homeless people and down-and-outs who live in the area. It's a place of incredible contrasts.

I signed up at the Vidal Sassoon Academy in Santa Monica and did an advanced course in colour. It's always important to keep fresh and up to date in hairdressing, no matter how successful you get. It's like giving yourself an MOT, especially if you're working in a salon that does not have a training school of its own. But this time my motivation was to get some ideas about working in America.

The first thing I learnt was that no matter how amazing a hairdresser you are, in the US you need to pass the State Board exam in 'cosmetology' before you can even wash a client's hair. Knowing how bad the American reputation for hairdressing is, you'd think this would be something a skilled British hairdresser could do with their eyes shut. Luckily for me, Morag's sister, Wendy, who used to be a manager at the Steiner salon in

Edinburgh, gave me the low-down on the dreadful State Board. She had failed the exam three times, and I met many others who were on their second attempt.

A cosmetology exam doesn't just include hair; you need to do make-up, acrylic and real nails, and facial and Afro-Caribbean hair as well as Caucasian. They even had a set way of cutting hair, and the daring Sassoon technique did not shine as well with the Board.

Some years later I met a truly gifted hairdresser, Massimo, when I was working in the stunning town of La Jolla, within the northern city limits of San Diego. He and his best friend Alfonso had both moved there from Naples in Italy, but try as he might, Massimo just could not pass the State Board exam. It was mainly through nerves and not realising that the exam is more about health and safety than being one of the best blow-driers in town. Morag modelled for him and, as he was a good mate of mine, she told me his little hands were shaking so hard she wanted to hug him. Despite not passing the exam, he kept working in the salon. However, there's one thing you can be sure about in the States: someone will report you if you are working illegally or aren't licensed. It's only a matter of time, especially if you're good at the job. Since the time of the early settlers in the Wild West, it's been every man for himself in America. Others will get jealous and want you out.

And so it happened that in the middle of a blow-dry, the State Board walked in on Massimo. He spotted them immediately and grabbed an American hairdresser to take over his client while he hid in the cupboard. She couldn't blow-dry to save her life and the client started to create, demanding that the girl get Massimo. Before she could though, the State Board representative stopped her and asked whether this was her client and told her that if she lied she could lose her licence. 'No, sir, this is not my client,' she said in her Texas accent as though she was in a court of law. The salon was fined and the State Board warned they would be back and if the Italian was working there, they would close down the shop.

The colouring course taught me nothing new. I stayed on and did the advanced cutting course to learn more about hairdressing in the US. The instructor, a good-looking Yorkshireman, kicked off by saying he had given up washing his hair every day and now washed it every other week instead. Every time he bent over to show me something it was killing me not to point out that there was a very good reason he should wash his hair every day – his head stank. We had a falling out over a lovely girl who had straightened Afro hair. She was really upset when I finished her hair – not with the cut, which she loved – but because the instructor told me to either natural dry it or use a Denman brush. But I knew that would have looked terrible; there was no way it was going to work. I had some hot irons and a round brush and finished it with those so she was happy. The instructor, though, was most put out; you'd have thought I'd tried to shoot him!

We planned to open up a salon in San Diego as friends told me it was going to be the new LA. Never listen to anyone who tells you an area is 'the new', as it's never as good as the old. I kissed goodbye to Morag and Santa Monica and rented a flat in University City, not far from the centre of San Diego. I applied for my California licence and went to an American school of cosmetology to study for the month leading up to the exam. Most of the students were on the one-year course required to take the exam. To take the State Board you need to have completed the course and prove that you have spent the hours (1,600 in total) hairdressing. People from outside California need to prove they have either been to a school of cosmetology or completed the hours, and as I'd been hairdressing for seven years, I qualified. But for anyone moving to the US, it would be advisable to go to an old-fashioned beauty school to learn about the State Board.

My two teachers at the school looked like the ugly sisters from *Cinderella*, hair-pieces and nails the length a drag queen would have killed for, together with fake eyelashes that looked like two spiders on an acid trip. On meeting them, I chuckled that they both badly needed a makeover themselves, never mind teaching beauty! They were a delight and chucked the book of cosmetology at me and set me to work learning new skills, which, on the whole, I would never need again.

One thing I did need to learn about was Afro-Caribbean hair. In the US, you need to do both, unlike in the UK. Afro-Caribbean hair may look strong, but, trust me, it can break off easily if you don't know what you're doing. Hair would often break off at the beauty school and people would laugh as the irate client looked at the mirror in horror. And some really painful beauty treatments were given out – I had my neck waxed by one girl and it felt like she had poured fire on me. 'Not like that, honey,' said the instructor, which did not relieve my pain in the slightest. But it was a great way to kick off getting to know the real America.

I am eternally grateful that I learnt how to do Afro hair. When I used to turn up to shoots with a black model or star, I could see the look on their faces. 'Oh God, silly white boy… might as well do my hair myself.' But they'd be really impressed when it became clear that I knew what I was doing. By not having that knowledge, you are ruling out a large clientele. Being an all-rounder is important, and it's also a big chunk of your State Board exam.

The day of my exam in Hollywood, Morag's sister, Wendy, agreed to model for me in the practical exam. You can hire models, but they often come from the street and it's not something I would recommend. Exams of any kind make me nervous and I was feeling quite sick so it was a relief to have a friendly face as my model. Renting your kit for the day is advisable for hygiene and practicality, plus you will never use most of the equipment again. And if you hire it then you can be certain that what you have is State Board approved; you can be failed for using equipment that's not in line with their specifications.

In the morning was the written section. I had spent two months reading up on the theory but my face fell when I was handed a multiple-choice questionnaire. Anyone with an ounce of intelligence and reasonable command of the English language could have passed and there was no need for me to have swatted up so much. Multiple-choice questions are like having a handy hint as to the correct answer, and even if you have no idea you have a chance of getting it right by shutting your eyes and ticking any old box!

The afternoon was the practical and that's the tricky part. You need to wear a white lab coat and have nothing in your pockets at any time or you'll be marked down. It's important that you keep the doors of your workstation closed at all times when not retrieving anything: it's all about health and safety.

You are given some cards with tasks on them, which you are asked to turn over. You then have to complete the task in the time stated on the card. My first task was to do an eyebrow shape and apply basic make-up. First, I had to have my client lie down on a table, tie her hair well off her face and then cleanse her face. This was the bit I feared most but it went well, until my table collapsed at the top, bringing Wendy's head down. I am accident prone, but luckily Wendy held still as I pushed the top of the table back into place. The examiner didn't seem to notice.

Next, to my horror, I turned over a card instructing me to do a manicure and one acrylic nail application. The manicure went well, mainly due to the fact that I had taken a week's course in nails before I left London. However, the acrylic nail looked has if I'd stuck a large wart on the end of her finger. The examiner looked at my model's hands, her eyebrow lifting, and when she saw the wart-like finger she made no comment.

It was a relief that my next task was to demonstrate a hot iron treatment, which meant I was back at a salon station where I felt more at home. The bad news was that I was sharing cupboards and drawers with a moaning, gum-chewing American woman who kept leaving the drawers and cupboards open. I was getting fed up as I knew this could mean an instant fail, so I waited till she did it yet again and, when the examiner was in earshot, I loudly asked her to please keep them shut, and closed one for her.

My model, being an ex-hairdresser and typical Scotswoman, could not keep quiet during the exam. She kept pointing at other students: 'Steven, have you seen what she is doing? She's got no hope,' she would tell me, and as the examiner went past she complimented me loudly on what I was doing. The exam seemed to fly by and we were asked to wait for our results.

All the passes were called out first and I was getting nervous, as the prospect of retaking and delaying my plans to work in the US was not appealing. It was a very long 20-minute wait until they got to my name – I'd passed! As I was leaving, I bumped into the woman who was working next to me. She had failed.

The following weekend was a time to celebrate and, as Martin was still in the UK and I'd been given an introduction to a wonderful rancher called Vern Magnusson, I was thinking horses and cattle. It was quite funny when he took me out to see his avocado ranch. He also had the most beautiful beach house in Carlsbad and was near a generator, which made the sea water a little warmer. Vern took me to meet two of the late Rock Hudson's friends, Al Roberts and Ken Jillson, at their home in Laguna Beach. It's home to the famous Pageant of the Masters festival, and is a truly breathtaking town. Once a year the two hosts held the most amazing AIDS benefit party.

The party Vern took me to was a small gathering in one of the most stunning homes I have ever seen. The living room looked down on their stone pool, surrounding hills and the nearby beach. The party was full of talk about Rock's former lover, Marc Christian, who was suing the Hudson Estate, and of him being out for whatever he could get.

Here I discovered that such things as 'A-', 'B-' and 'C-list' parties do exist. One guest, who often worked as a bartender at these parties, would work naked and stir your drink with his huge twelve-inch penis if it was requested. On this occasion, he was there in a non-professional capacity, although he did offer to demonstrate. 'The boys' parties are always the A-list parties,' he told me, referring to our hosts. I really don't like that kind of thing and I felt sorry for the people at the 'C' party. I had this vision of them standing round half a grapefruit with cheese on sticks sticking out, clutching glasses of warm Babycham. I had a great time – it was a really fascinating home, and it was not my last visit to Laguna Beach.

It was very easy to find work in a salon and if you are going to work in the US, it's always best to go to a shopping mall salon to kick off with where there are loads of walk-ins and passing trade. The salons tucked out of the way are usually run by established hairdressers, many renting a chair from the salon, and the chance of building a client list is slimmer, unless you are willing to advertise. My idea was to get hands-on experience working in a US salon before opening our own.

My first job was in a salon run by a lovely, glamorous woman called Christine, who looked a lot like Morgan Fairchild. Unlike in any other salon I had ever worked, she was not a qualified hairdresser. Her husband, an ex-baseball player, had bought it for her. What she did was to hold workshops on people's colours. This was terribly trendy in the eighties, and she would drape bits of cloth over people to find out what suited them best, helping them choose clothes, make-up and hair colour.

Within a week I was getting booked up, not just because my British accent was a huge hit with the clients, and my work was streets ahead of the other hairdressers, but because the colour seminars meant Christine talked clients into having new looks.

The second week there and I was completely booked up; one client even flew me out that week to Las Vegas to do her hair for her wedding. Martin had arrived and he drove there to meet me, as my client also paid for a room. I was excited to discover that the wedding was being held in the home of Elvis's former manager, and the bride had also invited Martin to the wedding. She seemed very excited that Martin was coming.

The first thing that I'd not been informed of was that it was a Hawaiian-themed wedding. The next was that she was hell bent on setting my partner up with her best girlfriend, who had seen him in the hotel lobby.

'Is Martin married?' she enquired. I could have said something but I was trying to keep it all professional. Martin and I were dressed in Comme des Garçons suits, a million miles from the Hawaiian look. Martin answered the door to two of the guests and they handed him their coats, mistaking him for a British butler. Martin couldn't wait to escape and we made our exit at an appropriate time, dashing back to the sanctuary of the hotel. Later Martin's suitor accosted him in the hotel and drunkenly swore at him for leaving early.

Once back in the salon things were getting even busier. Then I discovered that in the US there are immigrants from all over the world who in their own country are surgeons and doctors but now do menial tasks. I worked with a lovely manicurist,

Freda, who was from Iran. She was a qualified doctor there and was hoping to work in medicine in the US, but was required to retrain. She was doing nails in the meantime to fund herself.

Not all Americans welcome immigrants from the Middle East. One day I came across Kendal, a lovely Texan beautician. She was always saying 'God bless' to everyone and was in the back room disinfecting everything. 'I just had a homosexual in for a facial, honey, can't be too safe.' Before I could say anything she quickly informed me that she had booked two dear friends in and they were waiting for me at reception. She rushed me out and sitting there were two women who looked like drag queens – all smiles and big hair.

When the first one sat down, she was quick to say: 'Kendal says you're a God-fearing man.' I just smiled back. Then she added: 'I would like my nails done but not by that Freda; she's responsible for the American hostages and isn't God-fearing.' Well, Freda did fear God; just not their particular brand. How someone could be tarred with the same brush as terrorists, just because of their nationality, left me speechless. I'd never experienced such sad ignorance. I finished the two women and they just loved their hair, parading around the salon like a pair of peacocks.

Kendal came rushing in to tell me her friends were very important TV evangelists who apparently now adored me and wanted me to come to the studio to do them the following week.

'I am gay, Kendal! And I'm not a great Christian,' I finally shouted.

'Oh, I know that, honey! God bless you, but you're not the type of homosexual I was talking about. I was meaning the promiscuous ones you need to disinfect. I can feel God in you,' she replied. There are apparently two types of gay people in the US but I declined the invitation to go to the studio and do their evangelist hair, much as the shop owner tried to persuade me.

After just two months I left the salon looking to open up something more my own style.

La Jolla is one of the prettiest places in San Diego; we just knew that we wanted to be there. I felt sure with publicity and word of mouth I could make a great salon there. So we found an empty shell and launched the European Events salon. We should have bought a going concern, having no real idea of the numerous pitfalls of working in the States. The building work went well over budget and we should have included a clause that if the work was not completed on time we would be compensated accordingly. It ran almost two months over, costing a fortune.

Being overenthusiastic, I had all the publicity ready and had hired staff. My hair was falling out I was so nervous. Eventually it was all ready. A friend, Heather Campbell, joined me and three other hairdressers, a manicurist and receptionist. We opened, and after three months we had seven hairdressers, two manicurists and four juniors. The salon was open from nine in the morning till nine at night.

Anyone opening a shop in the US should join the local Chamber of Commerce. It's better than any magazine advertisement as it's all about networking in the States. I flooded La Jolla and surrounding areas with leaflets about the salon and refused to let any of my stylists just sit around; they had to go out to all the shops and buildings in the area, distributing leaflets and meeting the locals.

Then came the horrendous opening day party, which I chose to hold on the Sunday before a federal holiday (equivalent to a British bank holiday), thinking it would be great as everyone had the next day off. It was a disaster. Only a handful of people came. The woman from the Chamber of Commerce popped in on her way to a barbecue. A year later we got it right and held a party and fashion show early evening, mid-week; in fact it went so well, the police were called in as there were such a lot of people! Apparently we needed permits (as you do with everything in the States) and it was lucky that the event was almost over when they arrived – Martin was nearly arrested!

Everyone loved the fact that the staff all dressed in black and white and the TVs throughout the salon showed fashion shows. However, keeping the American staff in line was a nightmare. They just could not stop chewing gum and I was constantly having to remind them to keep to the uniform, even though T-shirts were supplied. We were charging high-end prices and I insisted that all staff had manicured nails, wore black and white and were well groomed. Much as they all loved the idea when they signed up to join us, I was beginning to feel like a tyrant trying to enforce the rules.

One staff member arrived in all white, but with her stomach showing and belly button piercing on full show. I did not allow any excess skin on display, including underarms. In super-conservative La Jolla, her look was a real no-no, and I sent her home to change. 'You look like you've been dancing at a night-club – it's a no,' I said. She left in a sulk and never returned, but sent a letter telling me she was suing me for calling her a lap dancer. She didn't take it any further.

Tips were also incredible in the US. Tips are really important when you are a junior – it's what you rely on to live, as your wages are a pittance. When I was a junior, we always fought to shampoo the clients as they would give a nice tip for bringing them coffee and washing their hair. Often towards the end of the week before pay-day, I was so broke I didn't have enough money for lunch and would pray a big-tipping client would come in before my break so I'd be able to eat.

As a stylist I have been tipped some seriously silly money. One client I took some time over, as she was having problems with hair loss, gave me a huge tip for what had been a $70 job. On finishing her hair I wrote down a few vitamins and a hair care system for her to take with her, and she seemed delighted. After paying at reception she came over to me and shoved what felt like a healthy tip into my back pocket and waved goodbye. When I went to the staff room to look, I found she had put five crisp new $100 bills in my pocket.

You can also expect to get some lovely gifts from clients over the holiday periods, especially if you take time over their hair and look after them properly. I've had watches, gold chains and even an MP3 player.

Clients in the US tip much better than in the UK – they tend not to work out the percentage, as in a restaurant, and on a $70 haircut the average tip would be anything from $10 to $17. If you are the owner of a salon, clients often don't tip, which is a shame really, as often the owner, with all the overheads of the salon, needs the money just as much as the stylist or the junior.

But really I would prefer that my clients just pay their bill and are happy, and perhaps bung the junior or assistant a few quid rather than worry about tipping me. Many of my clients are personal friends, and the fact that they are forking out for their hair what it might cost to buy a pair of designer shoes is enough. The best tip I could receive is to see them leave the salon looking happy and gorgeous.

My favourite member of staff was a girl called Wendy. I would never normally have taken her on, as she just wasn't the type that we wanted in the salon. She arrived at the interview and talked her head off; nothing I told her about dressing for the salon (she was in a denim skirt and low-cut top) seemed to put her off. As she left, she handed me a list of clients for the next day and said she couldn't wait to get started. There are some very talented hairdressers who never do well because they lack personality but Wendy was the opposite: an average hairdresser who talked her clients into anything she wanted, and she was always booked three weeks ahead. She worked hard though and appreciated our vision. It taught me not to judge a book by its cover.

I employed a very good-looking man as a junior who also worked as an exotic dancer. Everyone loved him, but by week two there was a problem. The girls came giggling into the back room, asking me to go look at him washing the client's hair. My back washes allowed the washer to stand behind the client and at first I was bemused as to what the problem was. Then I saw it – he had no underwear on and his penis was hanging down like a large club! No wonder he was a stripper. Not knowing quite how to deal with this, I went and bought him some Calvin Kleins and suggested he wore them. He laughed – he already had boxers on!

Then there was the workman's compensation policy you need to take out at great expense in the US; and it goes up every time you make a claim. To make sure there were no accidents on the salon floor, staff were asked to wear flat shoes. One night, after we washed the salon floor, one of my female employees went flying in four-inch stilettos, sliding onto her bottom. I took her straight to the doctor, who said she was fine, just a little bruising. Next day she phoned in sick and had found another doctor to say she'd ruptured her spleen in four places. It cost us a fortune.

A junior who I was planning to get rid of at the end of the month, as she was only being used for errands and cleaning up, nipped out to get some washing powder and, instead of using the pedestrian crossing, ran into the road and was hit by a truck. Much as I was genuinely upset about the incident, my dismay deepened when I discovered that as she was on a work errand we were liable. She was off work on full pay for six months and we had to cover all the hospital costs. Plus we had to take her back for a further six months when she was better. This was just two of the accidents that pushed our workman's comp through the roof.

Then I made a huge mistake. You can never pay any staff member more than 50 per cent of what they take in the salon otherwise you'll never make a profit. Panicking about money coming in and under pressure, I made a foolish deal with a popular local hairdresser, allowing him to rent the station at the bottom of the salon. He agreed to all the rules and a weekly rental, plus no commission on product sales; he also agreed not to let the others know he was doing booth rental. Stupidly, I committed to a year's rental under contract. I thought it might take some pressure off me, but it was my biggest mistake and caused nothing but upset till the bitter end.

It was not long before the other staff discovered he was renting and they demanded a commission increase. They all became unhappy and a few left. It was impossible to keep our stock separate from his and I would constantly find him taking our products. Whenever I confronted him, he would promise it was just a loan. The salon manager/receptionist became his best friend; when my back was turned he got her in his chair and gave her a new hair-do. So despite me telling her not to book any new clients or walk-ins to him, she gave him the work that should have gone to the hired staff. Eventually I had to let her go to stop the salon takings going down even further.

I was fully booked and had some of La Jolla's finest coming to me, including the former Mr California, Rick Stevenson, who ran Gold's Gym and sent all his members to me. I even had one woman who had seen one of my clients' hair in Las Vegas. She would fly in from Dallas on a private jet every six weeks. But by now I hated hairdressing, having become a babysitter for 15 unruly staff. On paper, with the car park full of BMWs and Jaguars, I should have been running a successful business but that was far from how things were.

I had to admit that, much as my talents were in hair, marketing and public relations, and though it was true that I could pack a

61

salon, when it came to business skills I was near the bottom of the class. My British management techniques were just not working.

And so, sadly, after three years, we were swamped with work comp claims (many of them false), huge tax bills and spiralling salary costs. There was no way out: we had to close. The only joy was seeing the look on the face of the booth rental guy when he threatened to sue. I just smiled and told him to do his worst. Maybe I was too young, but I look at salons now that mirror our image. You can't cry over spilt milk; but it was nearly the end of my American dream.

5

You Are My Brother

There's one thing to be said about a hot climate — it sure makes your problems seem a little smaller. As we sat outside our beautiful canyon home, a stone's throw from the exclusive La Costa resort golf course, a soft, humid wind was blowing and the sun beat down on our faces. At our feet was Costa, our diva of a cocker spaniel, named after the resort — and because she cost a lot.

Everything we had touched in the US had been a disaster. First there was the salon and then the beautiful home that Martin had spent a year renovating. He had created a European-style interior with hand-finished painting as well as drag and stipple paintwork. The result was a classy and elegant look but his work was sneered at by US realtors. They definitely inhabit the third circle of hell, the first belonging to lawyers and the second, accountants.

'It is buy or die,' one lady realtor said to us while looking at properties. Sometimes they would phone stalk you too in their attempts to make you buy. They were equally obnoxious when it came to selling. Despite Martin's labour of love, the realtors were completely negative: 'What is this weird painting thing? You'll have to cover it in white or vanilla, honey, if you're ever going to sell.'

Unlike the UK, old homes in the States do not always increase in value and a home having a history is not always a good selling point. Brand new or nearly new is almost always preferable.

Our home in La Costa had been built in the 1960s and the rumour was that most of the homes belonged to the Mafia back then, as they liked to play golf and lap up the opulent lifestyle when they weren't out whacking people. It came with a massive indoor Jacuzzi, three huge bedrooms, two bathrooms and a stunning view of the golf course. We often joked to visitors that there were a few mob members buried under the floorboards.

The thought of returning to the damp, windy climate of the UK, having failed in our great American dream, filled us both with dread. We could just see the faces in Brighton and feel the *schadenfreude* as they oozed sympathy, asking how it had all gone wrong.

Our California lifestyle of sun, sea, sand and the great outdoors was not something we would give up without a fight. As Costa chased a kangaroo mouse that had scuttled up from the canyon, we laughed and decided it was too good a lifestyle for us to throw the towel in yet. We would give it one more go.

Martin set about painting the house vanilla, though I am sure it was mixed with tears as he painted over his beautiful work. Having plenty of clients still keen for me to tend their locks, I looked for a salon where I could rent a chair. The first place I took a rental in was run by lovely people but was dark and smelt of damp; it was a million miles away from the glamour of European Events. Even the sandwich shop next door had to be closed as it had been infested with rats, so it was not long before I packed up my hairdryer and looked for another shop to work out of.

I was interested to hear that two Europeans had opened a new shop in La Jolla and I hoped they did not fall into the traps that we had. They were Italians, and Alfonso, the owner, had stereotypical Latin looks. He was dark and handsome, with his hair so lacquered in place that it never moved, and he had steely blue eyes, a chiselled jaw and a hairy chest popping out of his shirt with a gold cross dangling from his neck. On our first meeting he hugged me like a long lost friend and introduced me to his sidekick, Massimo. He told me in strictest confidence that Massimo was the greatest hairdresser but working illegally in the States as he had not passed his exams. Alfonso knew he could trust me, as I was 'not one of those stupid American hair-dressers'.

He got even more excited when he heard that, like him, my blow-dry technique was European. He soon introduced me to his lovely wife, a stunning American called Nancy. They were looking for staff and a deal was quickly made; I would start the following Thursday. But the night before, Nancy rang to say they could not take me on rental as it would look bad for the busi-ness, so instead we agreed on a large commission percentage, and I went ahead, having already told my eagerly awaiting clients to come there the next day.

The Italians were a delight to work for; they even bought me gifts on my first day, as well as putting flowers on my work-station. Alfonso did little hair but managed to look busy; in between smoking Marlboro reds and biting his well-worn finger nails, he liked to have meetings or coffees, or simply stress out. He left most of the hair to the overworked and put-upon Massimo.

'He is my brother,' Alfonso told me, pointing to a sweating Massimo, who had not managed to take either a lunch break or a coffee break. 'We will be brothers too,' Alfonso commanded, putting his arms around my neck and pulling me into him. Watching the little Massimo working like a slave, something told me it might be best not to become a relative of Alfonso.

It quickly became apparent that Massimo was not in fact his brother, but a long-term friend from Alfonso's hometown of Naples. After only three weeks, Alfonso wanted a meeting, at which he told me he and Nancy were having problems. Biting nails furiously, he blurted out: 'I only marry her for the green card!'

Nancy reminded me of a young Doris Day – she was full of life and had no idea that Alfonso had only married her to gain a work permit into the States. Nancy and I had become firm friends and I even started doing her hair, as her husband claimed he never had time.

'We are brothers, better than brothers,' he pleaded. 'What do I do?' He wanted me to talk to Nancy and get her to agree to separate while still going through with the green card interview, or at least to tell him what to say.

Now, a word to the wise – the minute an Italian tells you that you are his brother, RUN! It has happened to me twice and you'd have thought I would have learnt my lesson the first time. But Italians can be very seductive.

It was not long before Nancy moved out of the salon and without her the dynamics changed. Alfonso wanted more meetings, which I had to make time for in between juggling my clients.

'We come here because my car blew up,' Alfonso told me, lighting yet another cigarette, even though there was still a lit one in the ashtray. The US was a long way to come because of a faulty car, I remarked.

'No, no,' he shouted, 'it was blown up.'

Alfonso had apparently come out of a local eatery in Naples and as he walked towards his car it blew up. According to him, the local mob were responsible and so he and Massimo fled Italy for California. Hugging me tight, he assured me that, as brothers, we would never let each other down.

It was not long before being Alfonso's brother meant setting him up with my model client, Clara, and talking Nancy into not pulling the plug on his green card.

Sadly, he eventually lost management of the salon and had to move quickly, taking over the damp, dark salon I had worked in before. Alfonso promised to do it all up and told me to be 'a little patient'. Being a brother meant you had to do many things for Alfonso.

One day he took me for a lunch with some friends of his from New York. 'He is my brother,' he said, pointing to a man at the table with a stunning female brunette sitting beside him. But of course he was not Alfonso's brother, any more than I was.

Lunch was pleasant and Alfonso did most of the talking. After lunch I was asked to take the attractive brunette to the salon to show her around as Alfonso had a private chat with his 'brother'. Later I discovered that I had in fact been lunching with the nephew of New York crime boss John Gotti. The nephew was charming but not someone I would ever have imagined having lunch with.

It was all rather amusing until I saw the ugly side. Alfonso was obsessing about a local man who had insulted him over his credit status in front of his girlfriend. He had been going on about it for two days. Unfortunately, as I was cleaning up at the end of the day, the man in question walked past the shop. Alfonso and I were the only ones there and he smiled and beckoned the man in with a friendly wave. Alfonso took the man upstairs into the private beauty room and came back down after about ten minutes, wiping his hands.

'Clean him up,' he commanded, pointing upstairs. 'You're my brother, sort him out.'

Walking up stairs I sheepishly pushed open the beauty door and to my horror saw the man was doubled up in pain with blood dripping down his face. I offered help but he pushed me away in an attempt to retain his dignity. 'Do not tell anyone, please,' he said, looking up at me. No police came and it was never mentioned again.

As I drove home it was clear that it was time to find a new

salon. But Italians – especially ones who think you are their brother – do not like you leaving their business. So at first I cut down my workdays, only going there on Fridays and Saturdays. This did not go down well, but Alfonso reluctantly agreed.

By this time Martin and I had moved to the beautiful town of Laguna Niguel and I found work at the salon at the exclusive Ritz-Carlton hotel. On my first day the man I was replacing charged in to pick up his things. 'Good luck here,' he said, 'you're going to need it. They are cunts!' The receptionist told him to leave or she would call security, but the incident made me a little nervous.

In fact it was a very pleasant place to work. Clients would pay double the amount to have you come to their room and attend to their hair there. Lots of celebrities stayed at the hotel and many came into the salon, or spa. Madonna had been there the week before I started and used the spa gym but so many of the hotel staff had crowded down there to get a peep at her working out that a new rule had been put in place – no one working in the hotel could be in the spa area unless they were there in professional capacity.

On my second day, John Travolta popped his head round the door of the salon to look at his hair in the mirror after using the spa. I asked him if he wanted a quick blow-dry. It was great to find Kelly LeBrock (*The Woman in Red*) in my chair; she was stunning and I just blow-dried her. When I finished she ran her hands through her hair and thanked me. It was a nice start to my week.

The band The Cure came to stay at the hotel and their deathly white make-up caused a problem for security as they could not tell who were the band and who were fans – they all looked like white vampires.

Early on a Monday the receptionist at the Ritz told me I would need to go to a client's suite in the club area, which was equivalent to first class. The client had her own rollers and I was to put them in and go back that afternoon. It was important not to ask any questions, just perform the service and leave and she would be needing this done every other day while she was staying at the hotel.

Arriving in the club area, I was met by a male nurse who took me to the client. She was sitting in a wheelchair in the middle of the beautiful suite, fast asleep. I gingerly put in the rollers, a bit worried that she might be dead. As I finished, a man strode into the room, looked me up and down and demanded: 'Who is this?'

He looked alarmed but once the nurse told him I was from the salon, and had been vetted, he relaxed and smiled and told me to carry on. He was the lady's son and I felt guilty handing him a bill for $70 to put in ten rollers that would take seconds to comb out. I did this five times during her stay and she never once spoke. On the last day, I brought her an orchid from all of us at the salon to thank her for her custom, but my gesture seemed to create alarm.

'What is the orchid for?' the son demanded. I went quite red in the face as I explained that, as it was her last day, we thought it would be a nice going away gesture. 'How do you know it is our last day?' he snapped. I told him that as she was not booked in again for her hair we had assumed, perhaps wrongly, that she was leaving. He calmed down and started reading his newspaper, murmuring: 'I see, thank you.'

I never found out who the client was, though the male nurses told me they had a private jet on stand-by at Orange County airport. It was the strangest job I ever had to do.

Juggling working in San Diego and Laguna was taking its toll; the journey was long and I was booked from nine till nine. On my way back home one Friday I felt so shaky I pulled over off the 405 freeway into a car park and just burst into tears. It was almost an hour before I could drive. It had been a really busy day and I had taken $700 home for the day, so I put it down to simply being exhausted.

Despite taking the next day off to rest, I still felt awful on the Monday. It was not long before I was diagnosed with glandular fever, and for once in my life I had to take it easy. There was no choice: if I tried to do too much I just fell asleep. It took almost three months before I could go back to work full time and still I had to be careful not to overdo it.

Martin went back to England to look for some new business ideas; he was fast tiring of the American dream. The week he left there was an enormous forest fire in Laguna, which forced the residents to flee from their homes. Costa and I were sitting in my car outside the town, wondering what to do, when the police knocked on my door. They told me the fire had moved direction and I needed to get out of there quickly, as there was a gas station nearby that could blow up at any minute. It was a nightmare – I ended up sleeping with my dog at a friend's place with what I had managed to collect from the house. Natural disasters are not something you tend to have to worry about in the UK.

The disaster with our own salon, and having to sell our home in La Costa at a loss were taking their toll on our finances. We were running out of money to keep the high life going. Martin, after his visit to the UK, decided he wanted to move back, and wanted me to come with him. He did not want to pressure me, as he felt I still had a future in the US, so we rented out the Laguna apartment and moved to LA, which is where we should have been in the first place.

The truth is we did not have the money to move all our furniture and get ourselves back to the UK, not to mention all the other associated costs, such as getting our wonderful dog, Costa, over there. So Nancy, who had become a great friend, lent me the money to move all our furniture back, on the understanding that I paid her back each week. Once she was repaid, I would return to the UK.

I knew that a stint working in LA, and in particular, Beverly Hills, would look good on my c.v. I only worked Monday and Tuesday in LA, first in a salon called West End, which was run by a colourist called Fernando and his make-up artist boyfriend, Robert. Soon after, I moved to Juan Juan on Rodeo Drive. My heart wasn't in it, though, because I wanted to come home, so I never really built a good clientele there.

While we were in Beverly Hills I became friendly with Billy Connolly for a while – we used to bump into each other regularly and would have a cuppa and a chat at Paddington's tea room. For some crazy reason I told Lester about this, and of course he was desperate for an interview with Billy; but I was not going to ask him as it seemed inappropriate. Jonathan, a colourist at the salon, did Pamela Stephenson's hair and over conversation I said I knew her husband Billy. Jonathan told me to get him to show me his nipple piercing next time I saw him, as he'd just had it done. I mentioned it to Lester in passing and the next thing I knew it was plastered over the front page of *The Sun*, sourced to 'a Beverly Hills in hairdresser'.

Everyone knew that I had journalistic connections, so they realised it was me. Lester denied it but confessed one night when he was drunk. It ruined my relationship with Juan Juan.

In our first month in Los Angeles and just before Martin was due to head back to the UK for good, we were woken one night by the most enormous shaking. It felt as though the whole apartment was spinning. It was 1994, four in the morning, and we were in the middle of a 6.7 scale earthquake. It would have been quite terrifying but we hardly had time to catch our breath. We just grabbed Costa and got out into the street. We were too scared to get the car from the garage as there was a risk of the building collapsing. The scary part is the after-shocks – when they came Costa would scurry up into my arms and shake. They came for weeks after the initial quake.

Martin left and it was like I had lost an arm. LA was everything you could imagine: the party invites came rolling in, mainly because I was still young and appeared to be single. But I felt lonely and could not wait to get back to the UK. A month after Martin left, I put Costa in quarantine, paid Nancy in full, boarded a flight back to London and kissed America goodbye.

6

Rock 'n' Roll Hairdressers

Being back in London after eight years in California was a shock to the system, not just because I no longer had to drive everywhere, nor was it simply the lack of sunshine, but the fact was that I was suddenly lost as to what to do. I did not want to work in one of the industrial salons, having to build up a new clientele under the direction of some manager on my case all the time.

It occurred to me that maybe I should change professions. Several people suggested that, with my eye for publicity, I should go into showbiz public relations, though that would mean starting from scratch. I met with Neil Redding for informal drinks at Harvey Nichols; he is one of London's leading showbiz PR agents and looks after French and Saunders and Victoria Wood.

Lester Middlehurst was thrilled I was back. Neil owed Lester a favour, as he'd borrowed a car from him when he was starting out. But Neil and I never really gelled. Fiona Duff, a wonderful Scottish PR agent, gave me some work experience, but I didn't get off to the best start, managing to mix up Paul Schofield and Phillip Schofield. Thus I set up a phone interview with a tabloid newspaper for Paul Schofield, the classical actor, rather than the presenter Phillip Schofield, whose new show we were looking after. Fortunately, the lovely Fiona found it very funny and did not seem to feel it affected my prospects of making it in the PR world.

Some journalists could be extremely rude. 'Good morning, how are you today?' I asked one provincial paper reporter. 'None of your business,' she snapped. 'Ah, not a good day, then,' I hastily replied. 'Would you like to do an interview?'

It occurred to me that though some of the girls in the office got to go to showbiz parties and the like, it was often straight from work with very little time to get ready, and unless they owned the PR company the money seemed very poor. I could earn up to as $500 a day in the States doing hair. Much as I was getting better at writing press releases and coming up with ideas, I was not great at cold calling. By the end of the week, all the girls in the office looked great as I had worked my magic with their hair, and I decided that much as I liked PR, being poor was not for me.

Sitting in Knightsbridge's trendy coffee shop Patisserie Valerie, I flicked through the *Evening Standard* looking for jobs. One of the main stories was about Princess Diana joining the shampoo and set brigade. It was all about her changing hairdressers and joining the Knightsbridge celebrity hairdresser Gavin Hodge at the legendary Sweeny's salon.

You have to be careful to remember when you start doing hair for celebrities that they are the star, not you. There are a few hairdressers who end up becoming part of the glittering celebrity world, but it's only a handful. Many young talented hairdressers try to keep up with the celebrity high life enjoyed by their clients but end up out of their depth or in debt. Or they just become huge bores, acting as if they are brain surgeons rather than someone who simply puts tin foil in people's hair.

There was one young colourist I took a shine to as I could see a bit of me in him and I helped him with advice. He grew up on a council estate and did incredibly well, working in one of the best salons in town just a year after becoming established. But he turned into a total monster, snapping at juniors, never saying please or thank you and having diva fits all over the place. Many of his colleagues who were friends dropped him, he started taking drugs, and his work began to slide. He ended up seriously ill and in therapy, which really upset me but did not surprise me: if you begin to think that you are as rich and famous as your clients, it will only end badly.

Some salons give 100 per cent discount cards to lure stars in, but in my experience celebrities like to pay and to have their hair done quietly, quickly and discreetly. They must be able to trust you not to gossip about them, and you must be reliable and consistent. There are many hairdressers around who have celebrity clients coming out of their ears, but you'll never have heard of them; and that's the way most real stars prefer it. Some hair-dressers who boast about star clients will have looked after them only once. One hairdresser I know claims to have done Madonna; well, he did hold the blow-drier on the brush as the hairdresser styled her, and it was only once, but he still has her on his c.v.

Race Davies, an actress who played Jackie Owen in *EastEnders*, was a good customer of mine who had also become a friend. I noticed that her name was down as 'client' on a press release from a well-known West End colour salon. I mentioned it to her the next time she came in for her highlights, and she burst out laughing, saying she had been there only once and hadn't even liked the way they had done her hair!

On one occasion Denise Welch rang me to say she had been asked to go to a specialist colour salon by her producers to tone down her bright blonde, even though I was styling her the following day for an exclusive fashion shoot. She explained that the colourist was award-winning and that *Soldier Soldier* (the TV show in which Denise played Marsha Stubbs) was paying for it all. To be honest, having been Denise's hairdresser for such a long time, I was a little put out. As I was leaving the salon after a long day, I noticed there were three missed calls on my mobile from Denise. When I got hold of her, she was in tears, and told me she looked like she had been dipped in a pond.

When I saw her sitting on the stairs of my basement apartment, I did my best to be professional and not to laugh, as she was so upset. The colourist had apparently said to her, 'There, it looks in much better condition now.' A horrified Denise replied, 'I just want to look hot on the dance floor, and for men to lust after me. That won't happen if I look like a bloody tadpole!' I managed to sort it out in time for her shoot with Jeany Savage, the celebrity photographer, the next day.

Many hairdressers, when asked about what their inspiration is, say to have hair in beautiful condition or to give it great movement. I remember a journalist looking shocked when I told her what my inspiration is: When I finish a client, I want men to look at her and want to shag right there and then because she looks so good. Most women want to leave the shop and to see heads turn.

Talking of total bullshit in the business, I was about to meet one of the biggest players and most infamous figures in the industry – Gavin Hodge. As the Knightsbridge hairdresser was about to start looking after royalty, I reckoned he could use a bright stylist so I called him up to offer my services. I should have guessed that something wasn't quite right when Gavin answered the salon phone himself. I asked if he needed a stylist. 'I've not got any walk-in clients, but if you can build your own clients come see me,' he said, between coughs.

Sweeny's, based in a discreet basement in Knightsbridge's exclusive Beauchamp Place, was the rock 'n' roll salon of its time, and had not so long ago catered to such stars as Rod Stewart, the Stones and Marc Bolan to name but a few. The overweight Gavin didn't really fit the glamorous image of a hairdresser to royalty but I liked his obvious skill for publicity and went to see him.

I dressed up in a suit and bright blue Versace tie, thinking the smart look would be good for a salon that was about to host royalty. Sweeny's was anything but traditional, with just two wash-basins and a small stock room with a wash sink to mix tints, but the atmosphere was cosy and warm. Gavin was finishing a client when I arrived; there was another hairdresser there who looked as though he had been in a rock band at one time.

Gavin didn't just have a large waistline, he had a big person-ality too. 'No need to dress like that to work here,' he said, pointing at my tie as he lit up a fag and sat down by the salon reception desk. Having never worked in a salon where we even had a coffee anywhere near a client, let alone smoked in full view, I was taken aback at his casual approach.

He reiterated that he had no walk-in clients or passing trade, but that if there were any, I could have them. From experience, though, it takes forever to build from walk-ins and they are not usually the kind of clients you want, as they can be fickle. Hairdressers who just stand around waiting for things to happen never tend to do well in the business. So I reassured him that it would not be a problem, as I wanted to do my own thing anyway. As it turned out, Gavin only let me have one walk-in client in the years that I worked there. As I started to cut the client's hair, Gavin heard him telling me that he was a television producer and he almost spat his coffee; he loved anything to do with showbiz and would have taken the client himself if he'd realised.

Gavin's next revelation was that he ran a 'clean' shop, as he was in AA and NA and followed the 12-step programme, which was the bible for recovering addicts. Having lived in LA, I was all too familiar with the 12 steps. Over there, you have two beers and kiss a friend and before you know it you're standing up at an AA meeting saying, 'My name is John Doe and I'm an alco-holic.'

I just nodded and congratulated him on being clean, asking how long it had been. He muttered something and I assured him I never did drugs, they just did not interest me. So it was all agreed: I would start the following week, which would give me a bit of time to drum up some business.

With the help of Lester Middlehurst, who was by now working for the *Daily Mail*, I had some good, solid bookings for my first day at Sweeny's. The columnist and author, Jane Moore, a mutual friend of Lester's and mine, was my last client of the day and she came straight from working at her new job at *The Sun*. I offered to do Jane's hair for free as long as she would tell people about me but she would not hear of it and insisted on paying.

Jane was thrilled with her new colour. Gavin said how nice it was, and he took off into the back room with a male friend, leaving Jane and me alone on the salon floor. As I finished Jane's hair, Gavin reappeared, beckoning us into the back room. 'Either of you want a line?' he asked, referring to cocaine. Jane looked up from her magazine, lifted an eyebrow and replied, 'No thanks,' as if she had been asked whether she wanted sugar in her tea. I wasn't quite so cool – I was absolutely outraged and my face went bright red. I just about managed to mutter, 'Not for me.'

I quickly apologised to Jane but she was too busy admiring her hair. She seemed to find it rather amusing and never made any references to the incident.

I confronted Gavin, not just because of his outrageous behaviour towards my client but because of his previous – and obviously false – declaration that he was in the 12-step programme and that he ran a drug-free salon. 'I am clean,' he maintained. 'Coke is not my drug of choice, heroin was, but I haven't done it for years.' He smiled and patted me on the back, handed me a key to the salon and took off to the pub with his friend.

The friend, who worked as a dry-cleaner, was a regular visitor to the shop. As well as delivering Gavin's dry-cleaning, he brought drugs for Gavin and some of his wealthy Chelsea clients and friends. I remember a former model bouncing her young son on her knee and as Gavin blow-dried her hair, asking him: 'Gavin, is it nearly here, darling?' Ten minutes later the dealer arrived and she went on her way.

I stood alone in the salon feeling totally deflated. I wasn't sure what to do; the salon was perfect apart perhaps from needing a lick of paint, and I now had a key, which allowed me to work night and day and effectively meant I was self-employed. Also there was something instantly likeable about Gavin, and I reckoned that as long as I put him straight about ever offering any of my future clients lines of charlie – just stick to the traditional tea and coffee – it might be a dream come true.

Pretty soon, I discovered that Gavin doing Princess Diana's hair was 'a misunderstanding'. Apparently, an over-zealous journalist (who just happened to be a friend of Gavin) had heard a rumour and printed the story. Gavin had met the Princess through a mutual friend at a *Tatler* party and that friend was now annoyed with Gavin, believing him to be the source of the story. Gavin assured me that Diana had called him personally and was just fine about it; she knew that Gavin was not trying to profit from their friendship. He said she called him often for a little chat, although in the time I was there I never heard him take a call from her.

However, it is true to say that it was the salon of choice for some members of the Royal family – specifically, Viscount Linley and his wife Serena Linley. David Linley often used to cycle to the salon and slip in discreetly to have his hair done, not by Gavin, though, but by Gregg Taylor, the man that looked like he had been in a rock band.

The only time there was any fuss was the day that Gavin got his hands on Serena's hair. He could not believe his luck, as Gregg was on holiday and Serena needed a quick blow-dry as she was attending a function. Gregg is Sassoon trained and, though he is a nice cutter and blow-drier, hair up was not his forte. Gavin saw his opportunity to steal the titled client, and talked her into having her hair up, knowing full well that if she loved it, Gregg could never emulate it on his return.

I have never seen Gavin pay such attention to a client, although while her hot rollers were in, he slipped out and none of us could work out where he'd gone. As he lovingly finished his masterpiece, cameras began to flash through the basement window as the paparazzi besieged us. Gavin rushed in horror to shove cushions against the windows to block their view, delaying just long enough to allow them to take their pictures, of course.

The paparazzi were a familiar sight in Beauchamp Place, which was home to Princess Diana's favourite restaurant, San Lorenzo. The colonic clinic that Diana and many celebrities visited was also two doors down from the salon. But they had never before tried to take pictures through the small windows of Sweeny's – and what a coincidence the timing was! When Gregg returned, he asked the photographers how they knew about Serena and they confirmed what we all suspected – that publicity-hungry Gavin had tipped them off.

I met Princess Diana coming out of my small local gym in Earls Court one morning; I was surprised to see her and she really was rather lovely. She stopped and smiled and though I was just dying to ask her about Gavin I simply said, 'Good morning', and walked on. A few weeks later it was all over the papers that she was going to the gym, and she stopped training there.

My other brush with Royalty, some time later, was while helping with the Weston Spirit ball, in aid of the wonderful Simon Weston charity. Simon is the former British army soldier who was horribly disfigured in the Falklands War and has gone on to raise millions for charity.

He is a true inspiration to us all, with his positive outlook and enthusiasm and tireless fundraising. He also tells a cracking joke. As I had helped organise the raffle and auction prizes I was asked to the VIP area for drinks before the ball. Some of the so-called VIP guests were invited to meet Prince Andrew, who was one of the patrons of the event. Those who were lined up were searched by the Prince's security detail and we mere mortals, looking on, were searched too. I was in my dress kilt and it amused me that none of the security noticed that I had a bloody big skean-dhu (Scottish knife) down my sock!

My guest for the evening was the outrageous actress Nicola Duffett, always a blast on an evening out. To my surprise, Andrew suddenly popped up beside our small group, asking who we were. I think he would have stayed longer chatting to us if Duffett had not said, pointing at me, 'He works for *The Sun* newspaper and I'm an actress in *Family Affairs*.' We were all so taken aback as it had earlier been made clear that we would not be meeting him, and we had no idea what to say. Nevertheless, he was perfectly charming and did a great job that evening.

Back at the salon, Gavin's partner in crime, Gregg, was great to work with. Among his clients was Kenny Everett. Gregg had dated Cleo Rocos, who appeared on Kenny's TV show, but there was some bad feeling about her among Kenny's camp, and with Gregg, so it was best not to ask about her.

I had styled Kenny in Los Angeles for a photo shoot for the now defunct *Today* newspaper. Kenny was sweet, quite shy and terribly witty. Lester Middlehurst, who'd slept with Kenny in London a few times, had flown in to do the interview about breaking into the American market. Kenny instantly told me a story about having a threesome at his home, and being horrified when, as the moment of climax arrived, one of the men looked up and enquired: 'Did you get those curtains from Peter Jones?' He was a scream.

Kenny invited Lester and me to have lunch with two of the US promoters of his show, but when we got there they seemed a little perturbed at our presence. Not that it bothered Kenny, who was busy telling me that I was lovely and what a shame it was that I did not have a moustache. Men without taches all looked like women to him, he said.

After lunch Lester and Kenny jumped in the back of my convertible and I drove Kenny to the airport. He was flying business class and I suggested he might get an upgrade to first. Unlike Lester, who would always ask for an upgrade, Kenny was too embarrassed and told me not to mention it. But I got him all sorted and checked in. 'I should have one of you all the time, only with a moustache,' he declared, waving goodbye through security.

In my second week at the salon, Kenny left a message for Gregg on the salon answerphone, wanting an appointment, and I wondered whether he would recognise me when he came in. But I never saw him, as I was off the day of his appointment and, sadly, he passed away later that year.

I figured that I would hang out at Sweeny's for a bit to see if it got any better. Sadly, it got worse. Early one morning Sue Crawford, a brilliant journalist and former deputy editor of *The People*, was in having her hair done. I had just washed it when a badly hungover Gavin stomped down the stairs with a smelly McDonald's bag in his hand, followed close behind by his drug dealer friend. Gavin grunted at us and Sue looked up, but said nothing. Then came the sound of chopping from the back room, followed by snorting sounds.

Sue, though she looks like butter wouldn't melt in her mouth, is a woman of the world and there was no disguising the fact that Gavin was doing coke. Sue looked up again and her head turned towards the back room. Thinking on my toes, I quickly shouted: 'Make mine with sweet 'n' low, Gav!' Sue laughed and even Gavin had a giggle in the back room.

It was the last straw and I was about to tell him I was leaving when my phone rang. It was a new client, who wanted to come the following Tuesday. I hesitated over whether to tell her I would not be there but agreed a time and took down her number so I could call her later. As she rang off she said: 'Is Gavin going to be around? I hope so; it's a great cabaret down there!' Clients bored with the traditional salon loved the fact they could watch such bad behaviour going on around them while their hair was safe in my hands.

Gregg had a quiet word with me and said that much as he could not stand Gavin, it was a great place to work compared with somewhere you'd be reprimanded if you were ten minutes late. That certainly wasn't a problem at Sweeny's. But he told me to watch my back with Gavin.

So I let the cabaret continue and went about building a strong clientele. If they were famous or in journalism, Gavin would be all over them; he would even help you out if you were behind. If they were no use to Gavin you could have five clients in at once and he would go to the pub rather than lift a finger to help.

One day I was looking after Lauren Booth, Tony Blair's sister-in-law. I had just washed the colour off her hair and was in the back room mixing up some gloss to put over it. Gavin had taken half an E that morning so was particularly annoying. When I walked out, he was busy blow-drying her hair, and looked shocked when I didn't appear to be grateful!

Mind you, I once took over one of Gavin's clients halfway through her highlights – after he got bored, left for the pub for a 'quick' drink and never came back! But the golden rule is that you never touch anyone else's clients unless you are asked.

The PR agent, Andy Wigmore, asked me to do Lauren's hair the first time, claiming she was doing an article for *The Mirror* and that I would be credited in the paper if I did it for free.

Andy was a great guy and came through on a shoot for me to style Valerie Campbell, Naomi Campbell's mum. It was great fun; Valerie brought champagne to the shoot, which appeared in *OK Magazine* with my name for hair alongside. So when he asked about Lauren I agreed. Strangely, no feature ever appeared but Lauren had got her hair done free of charge. She had no explanation, but returned a second time and asked for a deal on her hair as soon as she sat down.

You need to be careful with some celebrities who ask for their hair to be done free for a shoot, saying that in return you will get a credit in the newspaper or magazine. If in doubt, ring the publication and check, just to cover yourself. Getting credited can be great and bring lots of clients in, but if it does not appear it will have cost you time and money.

I felt sorry for Lauren; she is an amazing self-promoter but sometimes to her own detriment. I took her and *The Bill* actress, Sam Robson, to the first ever Pride of Britain Awards. I remember that Tony Blair walked straight by our table and did not even stop to say hello to her. At first I thought he may not have seen his sister-in-law, but as the afternoon proceeded he made no attempt to speak to her at all. I cannot imagine ignoring one of my relatives at a do, though after spending time with Lauren I can see why some people would want to keep their distance – even family members!

The good news was that working at Sweeny's was paying off, and I was getting booked up. I also started doing lots of session work and I moved my clients to early morning and evenings, so I could fit it all in. I became so popular for colouring people blonde that it became a running joke among my friends: 'Stand next to Steven and you'll be turned blonde!' They had a point, as about three quarters of my clients were various shades of light. I really loved turning people into dynamic blondes and my nickname became The Blonde

Transformer. I rather liked that, and even my email began blondetransformer.

The fact that I was working in the salon did not stop Gavin stomping down the stairs in the evening with a group of young girls or the junior of the month. He had a habit of taking the juniors out partying with him and giving them the odd line of coke at work, which made them hard to deal with. If I did come in during the day Gavin would shout, 'Here comes Saffy,' a reference to Edina's strait-laced daughter in *Absolutely Fabulous*. Or, when I was appearing on GMTV, 'Here comes bloody Nicky Clarke.'

The only time I actually walked out was the evening Doctor Rosemary Leonard came down for her colour and Jan Roland, a showbiz lawyer, wanted her hair cut. I had asked Gavin not to bring his gang down, but I should have known that would be like a red rag to a bull. Sure enough, he came stomping down with some Sloane girls in short skirts. Luckily, I had moved my clients away from the front desk, but he started to talk loudly and then openly chopped coke up on the desk in front of everyone. After my clients left, I found him pissing in the tint room sink.

I told him exactly what I thought of his behaviour and that he had gone too far this time. 'You're not really welcome here unless you have an addiction problem,' I said, chucking the keys at him.

Gavin blamed my outburst on the fact that I had been in Leeds that weekend with the designer Anna Ryder Richardson at the Mr Gay UK competition and had had a bit of a time of it. That annoyed me even more, as I have never come to work hungover, nor have I ever had a drink with a client while doing her hair.

Eventually he got Lester Middlehurst to mediate, telling me he was sorry and would not come down in the evening again.

The salon would be mine after six. So I agreed to go back and for a while it was blissfully quiet there in the evenings.

Gavin always claimed he was the inspiration for the movie *Shampoo*, and although there was no actual evidence of this, people bought into the story. Having been hugely fashionable in the swinging sixties, he claimed to have bedded over 2,000 women, and to have consumed vast amounts of drink and drugs. He admitted to being addicted to women, and even in his later years his ability to befriend troubled young girls, giving them a fatherly shoulder to lean on – and a gram or two – meant he was just as successful with the ladies despite being troubled by gout.

Gavin had originally gone to work at Leonard's, which was the leading London salon of the sixties. In 1968, when he was 23, he made the front pages when he ran off with the debutante, Jayne Harries, who was just 16. They married in Gibraltar but she left him after only 15 months.

After that the heartbroken Gavin got on his motorbike and drove down to Marbella, where he opened a salon called Gotama. He had a daughter called Miranda by a Swedish model, Kirstin Wildlund. By his own admission it was bliss doing hair in the sun while also doing lots of acid. He returned to London three years later and opened a branch of Gotama in the King's Road. He married his second wife, Jan Burdette, in 1975, and they had two daughters, Candy and Gavanndra.

In 1983 Gavin checked into Broadway Lodge rehabilitation clinic and, for a while, succeeded in sorting himself out. He opened a chain of salons, including buying Sweeny's in Beauchamp Place. But in 1989, devastated by the death of his nine-year-old daughter, Candy, Gavin started drinking again, and his small empire disintegrated, leaving Sweeny's as his only salon.

There was no doubt Gavin was one hell of a character, addicted to women, drugs and booze. He could be incredibly kind and fatherly, but also cruel and destructive, desperate to bring everyone down to his level. I recall one evening when he had his dealer and a few of his girls down at the salon. He was at his most charming and begged me to stay for a glass of wine. He told me he was sorry he sometimes poked fun at me and that he thought I was great and a real asset to the salon. He passed me a joint, saying, 'Go on! Don't be so straight!'

I told Gavin I had smoked joints before but just not at work and he patted me on the back and laughed. I was actually enjoying myself but started to get very chatty and noticed that the effect of the joint was so different from any I had tried before. Gavin burst out laughing. 'Popped your cherry,' he said, admitting the joint was laced with coke. I was furious with him – I do not like being tricked into doing anything. This was the bad side of Gavin; we nicknamed him Fagin because of the way he would get others under his control and lead them astray.

Don't get me wrong; I'm no angel, and each of us has the right to make our own choices. We all have an addictive side to us, whether it's for chocolate or heroin; it is all a matter of degree. Daniella Westbrook once gave me a great example of addiction: she told me you could have ten people in a room, all of whom try coke for the first time. Four may never try it again; two might take it once more in their lifetime; another two might do it once a month; and the final two could be addicted within six months.

Eventually Gregg Taylor had enough and opened up his own salon in the spot where Diana used to have her colonic irrigation done by Chryssie Fitzgerald. Gavin was polite to begin with; after all, he had done nothing to help Gregg. But after a week I saw Gavin in his true colours as he started spreading vicious gossip about Gregg in an attempt to stop him opening. In the meantime, he was all over me and offered me a partnership on the shop in return for £10,000.

My business skills had improved since I was 24 and I made some enquiries first. It turned out there was no business to invest in and he owed a year's rent on Sweeny's. This was so Gavin and much as I had a soft spot for him, after he changed the locks twice so no one could get in, I moved to Gregg's salon.

Sweeny's closed and Gavin and I had some heated phone calls over the months as he tried to blame it on Gregg and me. But if he had just behaved himself, no one would have left.

My friend Lester Middlehurst tried to get me to have a drink with Gavin, who lived near him in Battersea. Gavin had really changed, Lester promised me; he had just seen him and he looked great, a changed man. But just as I was about to agree, Lester told me the reason Gavin looked so happy that day: Gavin had four morphine tablets in his pockets. So I decided to leave well alone. How many people do you know carry morphine tablets around with them?

Despite my differences with Gavin, I attended his funeral in October 2009, partly out of respect for his lovely daughter, Gavanndra, but also to honour the memory of someone who had been a true character.

7

The Sun Over Wapping

My first introduction to Jane Moore – during a trip back from the USA in 1993, shortly before I came home – came as a surprise not only to me, but also to Jane who, if she could, would have a placard on her front door saying 'NO VISITORS WITHOUT AN INVITE'.

I'm totally with her on that one but this did not deter the ever-determined Lester Middlehurst who charged across Clapham Common full of excitement about the prospect of having tea with his colleague Jane Moore, whom he said I would just love. It was not until he pressed her doorbell that I realised that tea had not been a prior arrangement, and that we weren't even expected. 'Jane hates unexpected visitors,' Lester said slyly.

I protested that maybe we should have phoned first, but Lester lit a menthol cigarette, took a drag and shook his head. Having been brought up with manners very much in mind, and being uncomfortable with surprise visitors myself, I was really embarrassed when Jane answered the door. Although she did not look thrilled, she invited us in, instructing Lester to put out his cigarette as her new baby, Ellie, was still up. When we entered the room her partner, James, was doing a portrait painting of them and it seemed we had interrupted a blissful family Sunday afternoon.

I felt uncomfortable as Lester, Ellie's godfather, waffled on about taking Ellie to Paris on her sixteenth birthday and tried to convince Jane that if he smoked at the other end of the room it would not affect her. Needless to say it was a strained first meeting and, as the next day I was returning to LA, Jane and I would not cross paths again until I came back to live in London in 1994.

This time it was a different Jane I met, one with a dry sense of humour, who called a spade a spade, and was determined and ambitious. She had just been to interview the lesbian comedian Sandra Bernhard, and had prepared for the interview by watching the video of Bernhard's new film and researching into the small hours. But the comedian had an attitude the minute Jane started the interview, refusing to talk about the film and insisting she did not want to talk about Madonna – though Jane hadn't even mentioned the singer.

Eventually Jane calmly asked Sandra why she had an attitude. 'Look in the mirror, honey, if you want to see attitude,' Ms Bernhard snapped back. Jane did not think twice and terminated the interview. She met Lester and me for a drink later at Number 9 Young Street, the bar opposite the *Daily Mail* building, and had us in tears of laughter with her story.

Jane does not suffer fools gladly, is fiercely loyal to her friends and is as stubborn as an ox when she makes her mind up about something. She had been working at *The Mirror* newspaper and had moved over to *The Sun* to edit the 'Sun Woman' section of the paper.

A few weeks into the new job she asked me to do the hair of socialite and 'it girl' Tamara Beckwith, for a photo shoot. She quickly filled me in, telling me there were some problems with the hair and make-up at *The Sun*. She could not do anything about the make-up for the moment but was working on it; and, if the shoot went well, I could hopefully do further hair sessions for *The Sun*.

It took me for ever to find Click Studios, which was *The Sun*'s studio of choice at the time. I had assumed it would be huge and would stand out a mile but that wasn't the case. It was a good walk from the actual *Sun* newspaper in Wapping and I had to call the fashion editor, Sam Howard, three times before I found it. We arrived at the same time and luckily she found it amusing, as she could see how flustered I was.

Click Studios were rather dingy, with a tired sofa in reception and a tiny galley kitchen. There were two studios, one with a decent-sized changing and make-up room; the other with a cupboard of a changing room. There was really no time to get too acquainted with the surroundings, as Tamara was already there. It was not a good start – hair and make-up should be there and ready to start well before the clients, just as they should in a salon. One of my pet peeves is hairdressers who are late.

We had a great bit of luck in that Tamara was adorable. She knew one of the salons in Beverly Hills where I had worked – Juan Juan – and we hit it off immediately. The make-up woman, Jan Wright, was the motherly kind and seemed really sweet, but a little anxious as to whether I did make-up as well; she relaxed when she heard that it was not my thing. Steve Lewis, *The Sun* staff photographer, also seemed lovely.

My first shoot with *The Sun* was nearly over, when Tamara's PR agent, Sean Borg, came charging into the changing room and decided he did not like the hair. He wanted me to change it, showing me a picture of how he felt it would look better. Tamara is very much her own woman and, thankfully, told Sean she loved it because it was so girly and she wanted it as it was.

The only other time someone charged in demanding changes was when the domineering Jim Davidson told me to change the wavy fifties look I had given his then girlfriend, Debbie Corrigan. He wanted a shaggy sex kitten look but it was more about control that anything else in my opinion. Debbie was really upset, as she loved her hair. But she did as she was told and seemed frightened;

Jim even told her what to eat, and as far as I could see she did nothing to stand up for herself.

I was laughing about it with the brilliant make-up artist Carl Stanley, who was working with me that day. Jim said he liked the make-up and on the way out he said sorry to me about the hair, adding, 'But it looked great in the end, eh?' He patted me on the back, then made a barbed comment about a mutual friend, saying that she 'was a fucking alcoholic'. I think he had been warned that I was friendly with this particular person and for some reason had it in for me the minute he came into the room.

Tamara's pictures went well and I was booked for another shoot by Sam Howard the following week. Ms Beckwith also booked me to do her hair for many a night out. I also did quite a few shoots with her after that; my favourite was when I got to dress her up for *OK Magazine* as Liza Minnelli, Clara Bow and Debbie Harry. She looked great as Liza; it took hours to razor the wig into shape and it fitted like a glove when I put it on.

The funniest shoot was at Tamara's home next to the Albert Hall in Kensington. I arrived on a Saturday afternoon and it was like an afternoon slumber party; Tara Palmer-Tomkinson was there, along with a bevy of beauties. I did five girls' hair in all, and once I had finished they stripped off, stepped into their stilettos, covered their derrières with designer handbags and posed for the camera. The picture was great fun and it appeared everywhere.

If you are going to do session work then you have to get used to nudity. There is no room for the prudish; I have even handed out ice cubes to models for topless shots to harden up their nipples and I once got on my knees and shaved a guy's legs and body. One famous Page Three girl once pulled out her boobs for me, lifting the right one to reveal a clearly visible scar from a boob job, asking if I could cover it. 'Would do, love, but I do hair,' I told her, and she popped them back in and strolled off, not in the least bit fazed.

Sue Carroll, the executive features editor at *The Sun*, called to say how great Tamara's hair looked and wanted me to do her own colour. Soon I was working three days a week at Click Studios doing the hair for *The Sun*.

It became clear that all was not well at Click. First I discovered that Jan was married to Steve Lewis the photographer, but did not want people to think she had been booked because of her husband. It was often funny when a celebrity would rant how awful Steve was as a photographer, thinking he was out of earshot, unaware that his wife was doing the make-up.

The lovely Martine McCutcheon didn't take to Steve when she came in to do a shoot for *The Sun*. She had done some slightly sexy pictures for the magazine *Loaded*, and *The Sun* was hoping that she would do something even more risqué for their pages. But, believe it or not, it was often difficult to talk up-and-coming actresses into wearing the titillating underwear or naughty outfits preferred by the powers that be at *The Sun*. We did once talk Melanie Sykes into a tiny gold bikini – it looked great, and she was about to do the picture when another photographer walked in, saw her and said: 'Cor blimey, give me strength!' Funnily enough, she changed out of the outfit quite quickly after that.

Martine was really nervous when she arrived and hated all the clothes we offered. She definitely did not want to wear underwear; I think she must have been read the Riot Act about saucy pictures by the *EastEnders* people or her own management. She was very sweet, and very pretty, and grabbed my hand, saying, 'I want to look more Audrey Hepburn.'

I nipped out with Sam and explained to Steve the look she wanted. 'Audrey who?' he shrieked, knowing that he would have to explain to the eagerly awaiting picture desk why she was looking elegant rather than sex on legs. I did her hair in the classic Hepburn style and she wore a lovely sleek dress and looked stunning. Steve was livid though and the atmosphere on the set was not good. She did not like Steve, and made that much clear when she came in to have her make-up touched up. She had Sam and me in stitches. Martine compounded the situation with Steve six months later when she came back into the studio with Daniella Westbrook and Patsy Palmer for a Christmas shoot. In front of Jan she belted out: 'Oh no, he isn't doing the pictures!' Martine is a lovely girl and always says hi to me at parties.

Unlike Denise Van Outen, who at the time was the weather girl on Channel 4's *The Big Breakfast*. When we shot her for *The Sun* she was really pleased with her hair, even pointing out to Jan and Steve how brilliant I was (they weren't particularly pleased as Jan had done the make-up). I then did her hair again on a few other occasions. A few years later I was at the opening night of her brilliant performance as Roxie Hart in the musical *Chicago*. At the after-show party I went up to congratulate her but she just looked at me and murmured 'thanks' as she walked by. I was a little embarrassed and wished I hadn't approached her.

The next thing I learnt was that Steve and Jan did not get on with the fashion editor Sam Howard, who was a delight. As far as I could see, if Jan hadn't been married to Steve, she would never have been booked to do the make-up, either by Sam or by Jane. That's one reason Sam liked having me there: I was on her side.

Click was by far the worst studio I ever worked in. Most other places had a selection of soft drinks and other things brought in but at Click there was tea and coffee and that was about it. Edwina Currie and her daughter, Debbie, were in for a shoot one day and Edwina asked me for a Perrier water and some ice. I opened the fridge, which had nothing in it but half a dry lemon.

It was embarrassing. It was nice work though, and I loved Sam Howard. There was something needy about Jan, though she did have a soft side and we got on quite well when it came down to it.

One of the hit shows at the time was *The Price is Right*, hosted by everyone's favourite wrinkly, Bruce Forsyth. *The Sun* was sponsoring the show, so Bruce's hostesses were regulars at the studio. One in particular stood out, the stunning Emma Noble. The first time I saw her I actually blurted out: 'God, you are beautiful!' The other two girls, Emma Steadman and Kimberley Cowell, were not too impressed with my enthusiasm for Emma Noble.

Sam Howard and I became good friends with Emma Noble; and Sam used her for lots of *Sun* fashion shoots. We would go out with her in the evening, once to the Formula 1 ball that Sam helped organise. Sam booked her as the F1 girl and we all made sure Emma was the model of choice whenever we could.

Sam invited Emma and me and my other half, Martin, to join her and her partner Ian Phillips on F1 team owner Eddie Jordan's boat, which was harboured in Palma, Majorca. Jordan was a friend of Ian's. Martin commented how stunning Emma was when he met her. She had little make-up on and was simply dressed; he described her as one of the most beautiful women he had ever seen. But poor Martin was not used to glamour models and could not understand why she was in the shower for 30 minutes, using the bulk of the hot water on the boat. It was then an hour before she appeared, ready for the night out. Martin was speechless. 'Why is she dressed as a transvestite?' he whispered to me. He had a point – unlike a lot of glamour girls, Emma does not need all the slap, as she is really beautiful. Too much of it can tend to make the girls look like men in drag, though it's fine on a shoot. A lot of the girls wear make-up as a mask to keep their confidence up.

Another time, I was asked to get some celebrities together for the opening night of the sensational Joe Longthorne at the Green Room at the Café Royal. Obviously the presence of celebrities helps boost publicity for events like this, and OK *Magazine* was coming to do a piece for its diary section, with the legendary Mark Moody doing the pictures. Of course as well as my usual gang, I invited Emma Noble.

One member of the club's management at the time was John Major's son, James, who was a handsome enough guy, but was never likely to set the world on fire. I think he was hired more for his name than his management skills. He was introduced to Emma early on in the evening and I think he blushed. Emma looked particularly stunning in a short sparkly number.

At the table with Emma we were having a real laugh. Mark asked her to pose with James for *OK*. 'I don't know, I don't really like Conservatives,' she moaned to me. I told her to go and do it as it would be great publicity and good for her, and so, smiling, she obliged. Poor Emma had little time to sit down that night, as she was the most popular celebrity to be pictured with. As I left, she was dancing with James, despite her reservations about Tories!

It soon developed into a relationship, which Emma tried to keep secret, even from me. I thought that was a bit rich, as she'd never have met James had I not invited her to the event. She was still keeping it quiet when she called to ask me to see her model for London Fashion week. Knowing most of the major players, and the locations for the week, I knew that Emma's engagement was only an offshoot of the main event

We got to the night-club in Islington at around midday and most of the audience were what you might call alternative. A picture of Betty Page was beamed onto the wall and there was a small screening of fifties-style fashion. The first model walked out in a corset outfit and stomped on a large dominatrix covered in tattoos. Sam almost fell off her chair and it was not long until a furious Emma Noble, in a corset number and looking like she was charging by the hour, came out with a face like thunder. The designer really knew how to put a show on and it was one of the best fashion shows I have ever been to. Emma was less than pleased, though, and we had to get a taxi for her as none had been organised.

The next thing I knew she had been bought up by *The Sun* and was under the wing of the PR agent Neil Reading. She was at a hotel with James, being interviewed by my mate, Jane Moore. I was really pleased for her.

At the time I was doing a lot of work with Goldwell hair care, and would use their products on shoots for fashion and beauty features. It was a great gig, as I got paid and so did the celebrity. Previously Emma had not been big enough to fill the criteria, but now she fitted the bill perfectly. So I rang her up and asked her to model for me. 'Oh darling, I am shooting with the *Sunday Times*, can you ring Neil Reading? Nice to hear from you,' she said, and then hung up. So, that was the reward for years of being a good mate to her and championing her all the way. Showbiz people can have pretty short-term memories.

I never bothered ringing Neil Reading, and the next time I saw Emma was on *Ready Steady Cook*. She had the same thick make-up on and looked amazing – but she had a new posh voice! Martin thought it was hilarious. The only other communication I had with her was when she appeared with John Major and was sporting new hair extensions. I commented in *The Sun* that she looked classier with short hair. She was not best pleased and sent a sharp message to me via Jane Moore: 'Tell Steven thanks for the comment.' It's a shame, as she is really a nice girl and I must admit I still have a soft spot for her.

Things took a turn for the worse at Click Studios when it came to makeovers on readers. I wanted to do the works on them, as previously it seemed all they had received was a blow-dry and some new make-up. I mentioned it to Jane and Sam, and they agreed. But the fact that I was a friend of Jane's, and had her ear, did not go down well with some people. Add to that the fact that Sue Carroll would pop over to the studio now and again to have me do her hair but never wanted her make-up done by Jan, and the atmosphere began to get distinctly frosty. But I got to do colour and full restyles on the readers and it looked great in the paper.

In those days the big buy-ups (exclusive showbiz interviews) were often photographed by other freelance photographers, such as Jeany Savage or Alan Strutt, rather than Steve Lewis. Gillian Taylforth, who was good friends with Jane Moore, had been bought up by *The Sun* even though she had lost a legal case against them. Jane was doing the words, and it was all top secret. I was to come to a studio in Camden on a Sunday and do her hair.

It is really important when doing shoots for magazines or papers not to talk about other jobs you have been on, or what celebrities you have been working with – and definitely not what the stars have said, or you could blow the exclusive. Also, if the stars think you gossip about other celebrities, they won't want you working on them. The Number One rule is discretion.

This was the first time I met the amazing photographer, Jeany Savage. Small, pretty and with masses of blonde hair, she speaks like Barbara Windsor and says whatever she likes. She did not get off to the best start with Jane, as Jeany asked her who she was. 'I am the one signing your invoice,' Jane replied frostily. Jeany kept pretty quiet after that.

Martyn Fletcher, make-up artist to Joan Rivers and hosts of other stars, was on the shoot and he was something special to watch, as well as being a top hairdresser. I felt quite intimidated. Gillian turned up and she was a joy, making me feel very relaxed. I created some really nice looks on her. Her husband, Geoff

Knights, turned up later and, although he was pleasant, he wasn't very likeable. To my mind, he had bully written all over him. My instinct was right – he came to another shoot and showed his true colours by trying to run things and demanding that Gillian look natural rather than all dolled up.

Jeany has a great eye as a photographer, and she gave me a great set of pictures. She never takes loads of shots, she just knows when she's got the one she wants and then it's on to the next shoot. There are photographers who can shoot and shoot in the hope they get that one special shot, and that means a long day for everyone else. Jeany's work is responsible for the launch of some of the greatest-looking girls in the business – Jordan, Kelly Brook, Nell McAndrew and Melinda Messenger to name just a few.

Jeany booked me for several other jobs, although I made a massive mistake when it came to Dawn Acton, who played Tracy Barlow in *Coronation Street*. Her hair was really greasy and I should have washed it straightaway but we were short of time, and under pressure we all make mistakes. Her hair-do started to drop under the lights from the second she walked onto the set. 'Bloody hell, Steve, what does she look like!' Jeany shouted. It was a disaster and I learnt no matter how little time there is you must never cut corners.

My worst job ever was for the *Daily Mail*. My darling friend, Lester, who should have been my manager, asked me to do a shoot for 'Femail', which was my first for *The Mail*. I agreed straightaway but then he slipped in that it was to do five beehives. 'But I can't do beehives,' I said. He was having none of it, however, so I sat up all night reading up on the sixties' hairstyle.

When I got there I was a nervous wreck and the journalist kept saying 'As a beehive expert...' I was far from being an expert but I was getting away with it – until another hairdresser, Mario, popped in to see the 'expert' work. But, God bless him, he never said a word, and I blagged it. So much so that, a week after *The Mail* article appeared I went on the 'Look Sharp' radio show and did a two-minute beehive for the presenter Liz Kershaw. In fact, I became a dab hand at it, which shows that sometimes being thrown in at the deep end is the best way to learn. It was all thanks to Lester's faith in me, though.

Another regular at Click was the lovely Nell McAndrew. She was really stunning but struggled at the start to get the recognition she deserved. Nell was easy to work with and would let you do anything to her hair. One day we were doing a fashion shoot using clothes from Cyber/Dog, a trendy shop in Camden market, which required me to dye her hair five different colours. I decided to use colour spray and that meant washing her hair in the kitchen sink each time, but she was a great sport about it and they were amazing pictures.

She really came to attention when she had to shave her hair off for a shoot in Germany. On her return, Jeany Savage shot her in the *Emmanuelle* style for the *Daily Star* and everyone went mad. Stuart Higgins demanded to know who she was (even though we had been using her for a few years) and said she should have been signed up for *The Sun*. But they had brought in a strict 'no implant' policy and that was the end of that, so *The Star* took her instead.

My favourite job with Nell was dying her hair yellow to match the Jordan Formula 1 car; her body was painted the same colour! We started at nine in the morning and finished with me dying her hair back at seven in the evening. The picture was worth all the effort though and Nell's career went from strength to strength, which is great, as she's genuinely as nice as she seems on television.

Some journalists started booking me to do hair, as it seemed the celebrities were relaxed and had fun when I was doing them. The journalist would sit in on the hair and often get some great quotes when the celebrities were off guard. This was fine, but sometimes it backfired as the more experienced of them always knew what the reporter was up to.

Lester booked me to fly to Paris to do Gloria Hunniford's hair. She was out there recording her radio show, and was going to meet the legendary Madame Bluebell of the Follies Bergère fame. When I got to the hotel Gloria was in the reception and I introduced myself, telling her I was going to do her hair the next day for the pictures with the *Daily Mail* photographer Jenny Goodall. Lester quickly intervened to add that I was not only the greatest hairdresser in the world, but also his best Gay Friend. Gloria looked a little baffled, as she had made no arrangements for a hairdresser, but since I was here she would be delighted, she said.

The next day I blow-dried her beautiful thick hair, which was a delight to do. Gloria has been around the block and I think she smelt a rat, particularly as Lester kept going on about being gay and how great our relationship was, and so she questioned me about why I had been flown over. Gloria and I went with Jenny to meet Madame Bluebell, who was a force to be reckoned with. We only had half an hour with her and two of the girls, and I had to put a headpiece on Gloria. It was a once in a lifetime experience, not only meeting a legend like Madame Bluebell, but being backstage at the Lido doing hair.

Next it was Lester's big interview, and the penny dropped that he was buttering Gloria up to do an exclusive about her son, Michael. Lester asked the big question about Michael Keating's sexuality and, as cool as a cucumber, Gloria replied, 'You do not know that I am aware of that, or if it's true.' She moved on to the next question, leaving Lester lost for words for once.

Much as the Paris trip had been one of my best, it did not leave me with a good feeling. I thought that Gloria may have felt that I was in on Lester's ploy to get her to talk about a subject she may not have been comfortable with. When I opened the paper the following Saturday, the first paragraph read: 'Gloria Hunniford's hair is a coiffured masterpiece.' Lester had asked me what her hair was like and I told him it was thick and easy to do. Three weeks later I bumped into Gloria and I was a little embarrassed. The first thing I told her was that I had never said that about her hair. She laughed and said she had no doubt I'd never uttered those words and squeezed my hand and gave me a little kiss.

Shortly after returning from Paris I got a call from Jane Moore. 'You're the new *Sun* hair columnist,' she declared. She told me to come up with some questions and answers myself for the first few columns and then readers would write in theirs. I was taken aback. 'But I can't spell,' I told her. Jane's only retort was that nor could half the journalists she knew, and that she would look forward to seeing my questions in due course.

That weekend was spent writing the columns, and I was nervous when I sent them over. Two days later Jane rang: 'And the problem was?' she asked. Jane loved them and told me to get Steve Lewis to do a head shot of me for the column. Steve reluctantly took the shot as Jan looked on. 'Nice to have friends in high places,' was the only comment made. The picture was awful but since it was due in that day I had no choice. Jeany Savage retook the photo a few weeks later and did a great job.

The only time Jane told me off came out of the blue. 'How do you spell Sally Meen?' she asked, after I had written how popular the GMTV weather girl's hairstyle was becoming. I had spelt it Mean, and I told her I had no idea. 'All you have to do is ring the press office at GMTV and ask them,' she said. 'There is no excuse for those kind of spelling mistakes.' She was right and it taught me a valuable lesson.

Funnily enough, thanks to my column I was a regular on Liberty Radio with Sally Meen and each Tuesday I had a guest spot talking about beauty, fashion, hair and behind-the-scenes gossip. Sally was lovely, but I nicknamed her Sally Me Me Me, as everything seemed to revolve around her. She almost made me choke live on air once, when I was talking about wheatgrass juice being the choice of top models such as Naomi Campbell; some even had colonics with it to give them energy. I brought some into the studio for us both to try, explaining to Sally that you took it like a shot. We counted down to five and I knocked mine back, only to see Sally screw her face up as she sniffed it and put it down untouched. I laughed so hard I don't know how I didn't choke. Sally was OK, but the show did not pay and the novelty of working for free soon wore off. The real upside of session work was the travel – and on one of my first travel jobs with *The Sun* I was about to find out about a completely different – and far more scary – kind of shoot.

Above:
Jordan – the infamous bunchies shot. (Alan Strutt/NI Syndication)

Above:
On my 21st birthday with a very young and handsome Lester Middlehurst and Natalie Megginson (my partner Martin's god-daughter).

Below left:
With Denise Welch in a real 80s jacket!

Below right:
With my partner Martin Annand and best friend Lester Middlehurst.

Above:
Denise and Sidney Born.

Below left:
When I first arrived in Brighton.

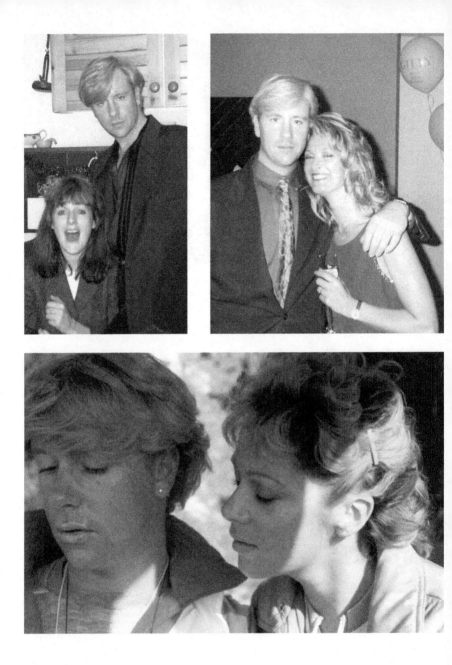

Above left:
With Jane Moore.

Above right:
With Gillian Taylforth.

Below:
Denise and me in Klosters.

Above left and right:
Pam Sharrock being transformed into an Anthea Turner lookalike.

Below left:
Ian Phillips, Sam Howard, Martin Annand and me with Emma Noble.

Below right:
Styling *Baywatch*'s Traci Bingham.

Above:
Me with model Nell McAndrew, Sam Howard (*The Sun*'s fashion editor), Katie Price and two soon-to-be reality TV stars: make-up artist Gary Cockerill (right) and DIY expert Phil Turner. (© Samantha Phillips)

Left:
Jane Moore and Lester Middlehurst.

Right:
Paul Gascoigne and waiter Francesco Alfonsetti at the Lennox Hotel.

Below:
Denise Welch demands yet another back rub by me.

Above:
Visiting Santa in Lapland with the When You Wish Upon a Star charity and a group of TV stars. L-R (back row): Grace Cassidy (*Emmerdale*), Matt Evers (*Dancing on Ice*), William Rush (*Waterloo Road*), Denise, me. Middle row: Chelsea Halfpenny (*Emmerdale*), the man himself!, Denise's youngest son Louis, Darcy Isa (*Waterloo Road*). Front: Sophie Powles (*Emmerdale*).

Below:
Jane Moore, me, Nicola Duffett, Pam Sharrock and Rose-Marie. (GOD Photography)

Above:
Pam Sharrock and Matt Evers. (GOD Photography)

Below:
Denise and me now. (GOD Photography)

8

Shot Down in a Hail of Hairspray

You wouldn't think there were many dangers in the glamorous world of hairdressing. Of course there's always the risk of being strangled by a hormonal diva, particularly if she's on stage in an hour and doesn't like the way you've done her hair. Apart from that, though, it's generally regarded as one of the safer professions. Imagine my surprise, then, when I found myself under fire – literally – and all in the cause of a photo shoot.

We were preparing to land at the exotic Comoros Islands in the Indian Ocean, where we were doing a shoot with the Miss United Kingdom, Shauna Gunn, before she entered the Miss World contest 1995.

The captain of the Emirates flight announced, in the somewhat understated way that pilots have, that 'something interesting' was happening. From his cheery tone of voice, I assumed there had either been a change in the weather or that he was about to tell us about some fun local festival. At least the announcement took my mind off the fumes that were wafting through the cabin after the crew had sprayed it with disinfectant.

Once I cleared the fumes from my throat, I waited along with the rest of the passengers for the next announcement. To our horror, it transpired that the plane was being shot at from the ground! A political coup was underway on the island and mercenaries had taken over the airport and all the government buildings. There were even tanks on the runway.

There was a stunned silence. This was not the kind of shoot we had in mind. 'Maybe we could do military fashion?' I suggested. Humour does wonders to ease the tension at moments such as these, I find.

Sam Howard was sitting next to me and behind us was Doris Tyler, the ex-wife of fashion designer Richard Tyler. Doris had a shocking cold and had been popping vitamin C and cold remedies all through the flight. The fumes had not helped her condition.

In fact, there had been nothing but drama since we left London. Shauna had arrived for the Emirates flights in a pair of bright orange hot pants. They were more akin to a strip of dental floss; even Kylie would have blushed. Apart from the acceptability of representing the UK looking like a lap dancer, there was a problem in that we were being sponsored by Emirates Airlines. As an Arab airline, they had a conservative attitude to dress and we also had a six-hour stopover in Dubai, a predominantly Muslim country where they take a dim view of indecent dress.

At the airport Sam Howard politely explained the problem and asked Shauna to change. The model looked surprised and, reluctantly, agreed to re-attire herself on the plane. Shauna, who was also Miss Northern Ireland, wasn't a bad-looking girl but in my opinion she should never have won Miss UK. There were plenty of shocked looks when her name was announced at the glittering Grosvenor House show; Sam and I were caught on camera that evening by the BBC, which was doing a documentary on the competition. We both looked thoroughly disapproving of the decision to give her the crown. There were rumours later that it was all to do with the Northern Ireland peace process and the view that it would help the talks if such a high-profile title went to someone from the province.

Doris had arrived looking glamorous and was clearly a woman ready to party. She was representing the London public relations company looking after Sol Kerzner's hotel group, which was sponsoring our accommodation on the Comoros. Doris's claim to fame, apart from being married to Richard, was that she was Britt Ekland's friend.

Britt has to be one of the rudest women I have ever met. A few years back I had dressed a wig for her for a pantomime photo shoot at *The Sun*. At the same time I was doing the lovely Lesley Joseph, who was professional and charming. Britt could not have been more of a contrast. I had put Lesley in a blonde wig, in striking contrast to her glossy black hair. I remarked to Britt how good Lesley looked blonde – at which, Britt stared at Lesley and simply said: 'I look good dark too.' When Britt's dress arrived for the shoot, it was the first opportunity she'd had to try it on. She was not happy and began to pull at the bodice, eventually taking a pair of scissors to it. She then snapped at me: 'Tie my shoes!' There was no 'please', no 'could you' and no 'thank you'. Her behaviour did not go down well with those present but I just gave her a look and replied: 'Certainly, your majesty!' and everyone burst out laughing. Britt seemed totally oblivious to her rudeness and asked what was funny? To be fair, she did give me a kiss on the way out and thanked me.

It was disappointing, though, as I had been quite excited about working with her. When I was growing up I thought she was amazing and really looked forward to meeting her. These days I try to avoid styling people I have idolised, as it's almost always a let-down when you meet them. They are only human, of course, and go to the loo just like the rest of us, but it is disappointing when they turn out to be unpleasant. It's hard for them, too – there's so much hype around celebrities it's impossible for most of them to live up to it.

So Doris's claim to be best of friends with the charmless Swedish actress did not impress me in the slightest. Nor did Doris's own behaviour – she grabbed me and babbled: 'You're gay. I love gay people, so many of my good friends are gay. We are going to get on famously.'

How wrong people can be, I thought to myself. It always gets my back up when I hear someone say that they simply adore all gay people. We're all different, whether we're gay or straight. I have plenty of gay and straight friends but I don't love all gay people or all straight people; I judge them as individuals, whatever their sexual preferences. There is good and bad in all people.

I know that Doris was just trying to put me at ease, but the fact that she was sitting next to me on the flight and sneezing all over me did not get us off to a good start. On top of that, she seemed to know very little about the location of the shoot and, considering she was the PR person, that was a worry.

Though Shauna had agreed to change into something more suitable on the plane, she had unfortunately checked her luggage in without getting a change of outfit out and was in the cockpit with the captain in her hot pants. Photographer Steve Lewis was snapping away, much to the horror of Sam, who was responsible for dressing Shauna and her general well-being. Sam was terrified the pictures would find their way back to *The Sun* but the Australian captain certainly seemed to be having a blast. Shauna could play up to anyone she thought was important.

At Dubai airport, during the stopover, Shauna's revealing hot pants were causing a commotion. Several men could be seen running to the bathroom to wash their feet and others headed to the mosque to pray after clocking her pants. It was suggested several times that it might be wise for Shauna to cover up but she was having none of it; flushed with her success with the captain, she simply thought Sam was being difficult.

There was worse news to come: our six-hour stopover turned out to be ten hours, as the flight was delayed. Shauna kept us entertained, though, if that's what you could call it. She was a nice enough girl but a little naive and was not prepared to listen.

As we sat in the lounge, boredom setting in, Shauna astonished us with the revelation that she planned to put her winnings from Miss UK towards opening her own ostrich farm. The birds would be reared and then slaughtered for meat – not exactly the sort of thing you'd normally associate with a Miss World contestant, and certainly not something you'd want aired in the media. It's generally best if beauty queens restrict their public ambitions to global peace and being kind to children and animals. Sam Howard, being a vegetarian, was speechless.

We were already exhausted when we got on the flight out of Dubai but the little local difficulty in the Comoros meant we couldn't land and the plane had to be diverted to Johannesburg. Doris, who was supposed to be organising the trip, reacted badly. 'What am I to do?' she cried, leaping up from her seat. That was hardly inspiring – if the trip organiser was at a loss, then what hope was there for the rest of us? Sam and I calmed her down while Steve called *The Sun* news desk to give them the 'Miss United Kingdom in plane terror' story. A vision of a tombstone with the words 'Shot down in a hail of hairspray' flashed through my mind.

When we finally arrived in Johannesburg we'd been up for almost 30 hours and nobody seemed to know quite what to do with us. A representative from Emirates suggested that we all fly back to Dubai and do the shoot there, but that meant another long flight, plus the weather was predicted to be windy, which would make a swimwear shoot difficult.

Sam was certainly not amused. 'With all due respect...' she told the Emirates representative (translation: Fuck off!). That was followed by a shake of her thick blonde hair, transforming the normally regal and elegant fashion editor into something more like Cousin It from *The Addams Family*.

Thirty minutes later we were in a people mover, heading to Sol Kerzner's Sun City resort. It was an hour and half from

Johannesburg, but our driver seemed determined to get there in under an hour. At several points in the journey I thought how ironic it would be to survive our plane being shot at only to die in a road traffic accident. There had been a series of car-jackings recently and the driver was keen not to stop at lights. Fortunately, we were mostly too tired to worry too much about the speed he was going.

Some 35 hours after we had first set out we arrived at the gates of the magnificent Sun City. It was breathtaking in its opulent luxury and a far cry from the poverty-stricken townships we had driven past. We were given keys to our rooms and Sam suggested we rest for a few hours before having dinner at seven, when we would meet the manager of the hotel.

I was so exhausted I couldn't wait to lie down but Shauna piped up: 'What time before dinner is Steven doing my hair?' I could not believe she expected me to start working on her hair after having been up for a day and a half. Sam burst out laughing, and told her to do her own hair; she'd have to do it at the Miss World pageant anyway and I was only employed to tend to her for the photo shoots. 'But he is part of my prize!' she wailed. 'I can't do my own hair!'

'Then you'd better learn,' was Sam's swift response. Shauna seemed to think that we were all at her beck and call and kept insisting that I was part of the prize. She was less than happy as she stomped off to her room.

When you are a session stylist you have to be prepared to work all hours. I am often up at 4.30am to do a client that has a morning television show, or if a photographer needs a certain light I can be up as early as 3.30am getting the girls' hair ready. You also have to be prepared to climb mountains and wade into water to do the job right.

One German company even asked me to glue a model's hair to the sand as she lay on the beach, as the wind was blowing it too much. Much to the girl's relief, I refused; photographers always want the impossible but there is a limit.

Next morning Shauna was sick with a stomach bug, so we could not shoot with her. One of the crew commented rather unkindly that it might make her lose some weight and help the clothes fit better. Most fashion companies send sample sizes for shoots between 8 and 10 but Shauna was a bit bigger than the average model and it was going to be a struggle getting the outfits to fit.

Instead we started shooting on a lovely Brazilian model we had brought with us called Christianne Gadd, who is now called Christianne Oliveira. She went on to star in *EastEnders* playing Carla Mitchell, and it was claimed that she got the part due to her strong sexual chemistry with Ross Kemp; either way she was a lovely girl. I was up at 4am so we could catch the light and had half an hour to style her. Meanwhile Janet, the make-up artist, was enjoying a leisurely breakfast with Steve in their room. She had no intention of getting up early to do make-up but as she was married to the photographer there was no arguing.

The shoot went well, though we could have been anywhere for some of the shots. We shot one on a bridge that might just as well have been in Scotland rather than South Africa. But Steve Lewis the photographer was happy, so it was a wrap.

There was bad news when we got back to reception. Shauna needed a doctor and was going to be laid up in bed for four days. Then worse news from Doris – the hotel was fully booked and we were all going to have to share rooms. I would have to have to bunk in with Jan and Steve; Christianne with the poorly Shauna; and Sam with Doris. Sam immediately insisted on sharing with me; she was not altogether comfortable with the flamboyant Mrs Tyler, and it was a relief for me too.

So, for the first time in years, I woke up in bed with a

stunning blonde woman wearing pretty pink PJs. Sam and I got on so well we shared rooms every time we went on a trip.

Sun City was stunning but after two days it was a bit like being locked up in Disneyland for adults. Sam and I were beginning to feel claustrophobic; we just wanted to get out and do a safari or something – anything!

Shauna managed to rally round and do one shoot, though we ended up getting more pictures of me than anything else! We were doing pool shots – the water hides a multitude of sins – but as I helped Shauna into the water I fell into the pool and soaked myself from head to toe. Everyone fell around laughing and Steve took more pictures of me up to my ears in water than he did of Shauna.

One rule of the trade is, if in doubt, just get them wet. It almost always looks good. Shauna did have the most beautiful thick red hair and when it was styled well it was her saving grace, so we kept that dry. After that one shoot with Shauna, her stomach bug came back with a vengeance, compounded by an insect bite she insisted was infected. So Shauna was back in her room again. Foreign jobs could either be amazing or just one big nightmare, as Sun City was rapidly becoming.

The next day Shauna was still not well enough to do photographs so we enjoyed a day off exploring. Sam and I went to see the famous alligators but got a frosty reception on our return. It seemed our Miss UK's finger had flared up and Jan had had to take her to the doctor. Jan's day off had been spoilt and she was now in her room having a massage to recover. Steve was less than happy.

We were invited to dinner by Sol's right-hand man, along with a relative of the movie star Louis Gossett Jr. We accepted but declined for the ailing Shauna. However, she somehow caught wind of it and made a remarkable recovery, arriving fully made-up in revealing, glittery top and, yes, you've guessed it, matching hot pants. She chatted and flirted with the guests and you'd never have known she'd been ill. My guess is that she just didn't like us and hated being told what to do. She wore the hot pants on the flight back too.

We weren't surprised when Shauna failed to be placed in the Miss World pageant. She was a pretty enough girl but perhaps if she'd listened a bit more she might have done better.

One of my favourite foreign trips was to Fort Lauderdale in Florida with the footballer Dean Holdsworth. Dean had been a naughty boy and had been playing away from home with the model Linsey Dawn McKenzie. After a close-quarters tackle on the bonnet of his BMW, the 17-year-old stunner was shocked to discover that the handsome 27-year-old striker was married, and tearily told her tale to the tabloids. Dean's wife, Samantha, who was busy reinventing herself as a pop star, decided to give the marriage a go for the sake of the children. *The Sun* bought up the reunited couple and sent them off on holiday in style – accompanied by Steve Lewis, Sam Howard and me.

Dean Holdsworth was a laugh a minute and an absolute joy to work with. Good-looking and a right lad, he was the opposite of his wife. Samantha name-dropped the whole time about her 'best friends' Rod Stewart and Rachel Hunter. Sam Howard and I used to kick each other under the table every time she mentioned Rachel. When she wasn't talking about Rod 'n' Rachel, Samantha was sullen and sulky, but then her husband had just been caught cheating on her, so it's probably understandable. They had brought their 20-month-old son, Jordan, with them and four-year-old Bradley, and Dean appeared to be a loving father. But I didn't hold out much hope for the marriage.

For starters, Dean was more high maintenance than his glamorous wife. After I blow-dried his hair he would like large blue rollers put in to add volume. They would stay in while he had his make-up done, sitting in just a tiny pair of blue underpants.

Dean could have given any Calvin Klein model a run for their money – and I would have been happy to put rollers in for him all day long.

Photographer Steve Lewis was also on good form on the Florida trip. For once he was not flanked by his wife, Jan, and seemed happier and more at ease, joking around and partying with Sam and me. Dean had us in the gym every day, doing football circuit training, and we all partied in South Beach, travelling in a stretch limo, dining at Thai Tony's and drinking in the Delano Hotel.

We only did two days of actual shooting with the couple and it was a dream job. Sadly, Dean punched Samantha a few years later and received an 18-month suspended sentence. You could not have seen that happening but then you never really know what goes on behind closed doors.

9

And It's a Very Good Morning From Me

Renowned Aussie journalist, Robyn Foyster, had become a friend in Los Angeles, where I had done her hair and helped her on one or two projects. It was Robyn who rocketed Morag Kerr to fame as the 'caterer to the stars' in a three-part deal for the now defunct *Today* newspaper. Morag wasn't entirely suited to the project; she liked the idea of the money, as she was tiring of the LA lifestyle and wanted to move back to Canada to be nearer her family, but when it came to the interviews and pictures she was like a frightened chicken.

With a little coaching from Robyn and me, her recipes and her file of A-list client stories made the articles a huge hit. Book deals and offers for Morag to appear on *The Oprah Winfrey Show* and a host of other talk shows, came piling in for the Scottish caterer. But, because I wasn't around to encourage her, the shy Morag turned them all down, as she was too frightened people would sue her.

I only saw Morag once after that, when she came to stay with me in London. Despite the fact she had turned down the chance of money and international fame, she had no regrets, saying: 'Oh, the paper thing was enough for me, dear, my nerves couldn't stand it. Not everyone in this world is fame-hungry.'

Sadly, a year later Morag died. She called me three weeks before to tell me she had cancer. 'Where are you?' I asked. 'In the Beverly Shopping Centre,' she replied. Ever resourceful, Morag had taken herself out of the hospital, hidden her colostomy bag in a shopping bag and was out taking in the sights with her sister, Wendy. Of course, she would also have taken the opportunity for a sneaky Players cigarette. She was one of a kind and is greatly missed.

Robyn asked about Morag on the beautifully warm day of her marriage to Jo Townsend. In fact, it was so warm that after finishing her hair and styling a few other guests, I looked like I'd run the London Marathon. It's always best to change after you have done the hair, not before. I really don't like doing wedding hair as there are too many people interfering and the bride is nervous. When I had finished the hair of one bride in Brighton she burst into tears, protesting that she hated it, and just cried and cried. But it was the exact same hair-do that we had tried out on at least four occasions prior to the big day. It's always best to have at least a few trials of your chosen hair-do. It turned out she didn't want to get married at all and the tears were nothing to do with her hair. The wedding did go ahead though and the bride didn't even apologise for her behaviour when she returned to the salon after the honeymoon.

Robyn was a calm bride and, apart from trying to persuade a bedraggled-looking me to join her in the car with everyone, saying that I looked fine, the morning went without a hitch. Legging it back home, I grabbed a change of outfit and headed to the Christopher Wren chapel at the Old Royal Naval College in Greenwich, which was one of the churches used in *Four Weddings and a Funeral*. I got there just as everyone came out to board the riverboat hired for the occasion.

Lester was thrilled when I got there, not because I was late, nor because the wedding had been beautiful. No, his excitement was because a mobile phone had gone off during the ceremony and the culprit was Jane Moore. Jane was always so perfect, so it had made Lester's day. Jane had laughed it off and apologised but felt awful about forgetting to turn off her mobile. Still, she was finding it a little tiresome the thirty-second time that Lester drew attention to it during the day. I was worried that I was going to hear someone yell 'man overboard' and discover that Jane had shoved him head-first into the Thames. Luckily Lester noticed that Des O'Connor and his now wife, Jodie Brooke Wilson, were guests and had moved on to try and make them his new best friends.

The boat docked at the River Café for a wonderful wedding lunch. All the guests were seated; Jane and I sat together with Lester and a few other friends. There was one guest missing at our table – the place name-tag was inscribed 'Liam Hamilton'. None of us knew the name and we all pondered who the mystery man might be. I joked that he was a wealthy property bachelor; when he did arrive I think we all felt sorry for him because we'd invented so many tales. Liam was, in fact, the former executive producer at GMTV who had moved on to become managing director at LWT.

We hit it off straightaway; he was a lovely, unassuming man with a dry Scots sense of humour, good-looking and to the point. He loved the fact we had all been making up stories about him and we became great pals.

After lunch we all climbed back on the boat and partied the afternoon away. The bar staff had never catered for so many hard-drinking journalists and, alas, ran out of glasses. Lester and I had everyone lend a hand washing the glasses and helping with drinks; even Des O'Connor did his bit. It was one of the best weddings I have ever been to.

Months later, sitting with Liam Hamilton over drinks at the Café Royal in Regent Street, he introduced me to GMTV producer Ben Frow, who oversaw the makeover section of Lorraine Kelly's show. I had my own column in Britain's number one newspaper, *The Sun*, and my makeovers appeared in the *Daily Mail* and several of the glossies, so Liam suggested me for the show. I was a little embarrassed at first as I felt Ben had been put on the spot, but then I thought that he simply wouldn't call if he didn't want to use me, so I just enjoyed the evening.

The phone rang the following Tuesday, and I was asked if I could come to the TV studio on Monday to makeover two women into their idols, Pamela Anderson and Tina Turner. A car would be sent for me.

There was no time to be nervous and the next thing I knew there I was, with two heavy bags in hand, in a studio in the city of London. Ben was not there, as he was the commissioning producer and primarily handed out the assignments. The woman who was directing the show was not very friendly to kick off with. 'Where are your people?' she asked, looking over my shoulder. It seemed that previous hairdressers had brought an army of assistants with them. When I told her it was just me, it did nothing to relieve her suspicions. 'You're not planning on taking the two viewers off anywhere, are you?' It seemed one celebrity hairdresser had taken a woman who wanted to be Madonna off to his salon and she had been there all day, delaying filming until late in the evening.

I put her at ease, regaling her with the story of how I had single-handedly done makeovers on eleven Territorial Army women in Portsmouth, turning them into débutantes in one day, while suffering from shingles. A mere two makeovers in a day was not going to be much of a strain, I told her, which almost raised a smile.

I was introduced to Canadian-born Ariane Poole, who was to do the make-up for the day. She is really talented and has an international reputation and it was a pleasure to work with her. She made me feel really at ease, telling me she could see I was a natural and she was sure we would be working together again.

The first thing we had to film was a staged 'good morning'

to Lorraine, even though she was not in the studio; many of the makeovers are prerecorded and then shown as 'live'. Then the viewer who was being transformed into Pamela Anderson appeared and we were filmed welcoming her, giving her a consultation and looking very enthusiastic about her vision. The viewer was perfect; a quick touch-up of her roots, a fringe cutting in and a messy blow-dry and she would be *Baywatch* personified.

There was only one problem – she didn't want a fringe, even though Pamela's sexy fringe is her trademark. Now, there are fringe wigs but I didn't have one with me and they don't look that great. I could have faked a fringe with her own hair but, as they wanted her to do the famous *Baywatch* run across the studio, it might have fallen, which would have looked terrible. It was important for me to make a good first impression, so I told her I would cut a tiny lace fringe that she could get rid of later. She ummed and ahhed for a while, then got caught up in the moment and agreed to my suggestion, so I just cut the full fringe in and she looked the business. It was a gamble but she loved it and thanked me afterwards; the producer was thrilled that it had all been done quickly, with so little fuss, and Ariane's make-up was sublime.

Not all celebrity make-up artists were as quick, laid-back and professional as Ariane. One very famous make-up woman was an hour late for filming. Moreover, her own clothes rack, loaded with more items than many celebrities have on a shoot, arrived on time in a separate car. When she finally turned up, she asked what the producer wanted her to wear. The irate producer asked her to just get on with the makeover. Put out, she asked for time to do her own make-up and we were two hours late starting. That said, the make-up she used for the makeover was incredible and she was lovely, if a bit full of herself.

Next up, after lunch, we met the viewer who wanted to be Tina Turner. I was well prepared with wigs in my bag and everything necessary to do Afro-Caribbean hair. The lovely lady who arrived had very short, straightened hair, which was plastered to her scalp with product. My comb is not a magic wand so it had to be a wig. The one I chose was a long wig the same colour as Tina Turner's hair, but it's hard to buy wigs that have the same volume as the singer's. So, I turned the wig upside down and put it on the woman's head. The producer looked worried but as I began to razor cut it short Tina emerged. Before I knew it, I was dancing to 'Simply the Best' by Tina Turner, something all my friends told me not to do again. It was five o'clock and we had finished and even the producer was smiling. Ben called and booked me for more makeovers.

Then came a very special booking: could I transform Lorraine Kelly into the iconic Elizabeth Taylor? Originally they had planned to fly Lorraine to Paris and have John Galliano's team style her. But, budgets being what they were, a team from London was being assembled at the Mandarin Oriental Hotel in Knightsbridge.

You don't really see it on the show, but Lorraine is one sexy lady. At Liam Hamilton's wedding in Italy, she wore a sheer pink dress that really turned heads; it left little to the imagination, yet remained classy and elegant. Lorraine is also incredibly professional; she turned up right on time with no airs and graces and I explained what I was going to do. My first thought had been to style a wig and I had it on standby, but I really wanted to use Lorraine's own hair. I used an old-fashioned black leave-in rinse that they used to apply in the old days for shampoo and sets. It made her hair very dark and it also made the hair sticky so it took on a different texture. I blow-dried it into the shape I wanted and then I went over it with a hot iron, applying hairspray to each section. It looked amazing. Finally I blow-dried the lot out, ruffled it up with my hands and dried the front a little straighter. I really fussed over it. In the end Lorraine stopped me in her sweet Scots accent, piping up: 'I can't believe it is my hair, I think you've got it, Steve.'

She moved on to get made-up by Ariane Poole. The unveiling of her final look, including pricey jewels with bodyguards standing by, was on the imposing stairs of the hotel. When Lorraine walked down the staircase it was a masterpiece by our team; she looked every inch the image of her Hollywood idol.

The other great part of doing hair on television is that you get invited to a lot of events and parties, in particular LWT's *An Audience With...* series, and I now got to sit in the celebrity section. The programme is usually recorded on a Sunday and it made for a nice evening out.

One evening – '*An Audience With the Spice Girls*' – was especially memorable. Prior to the show, I had been over in Wandsworth to dress Andy Coulson in drag. At this point Andy was working at *The Sun* but would later become *News of the World* editor and would eventually step down as David Cameron's right-hand man due to the phone hacking scandal. It was a brilliant set up: Andy was to go to the show dressed as a woman. He would ask a question and be 'outed' as an undercover reporter by the Spice Girls. He would then walk out in front of the packed audience. Sue Moxely did the make-up and I was in charge of the wig and dressing up Andy to pass as a woman. The make-up looked great as Andy has quite a pretty face and the wig went on like a dream, but dressing him up was another thing altogether – we had to get three pairs of tights on him to cover his hairy legs and then create a bust using gaffer tape and tights. Andy was hysterical and we were trying to protect his dignity while helping him struggle into the tights. 'Oh for God's sake, Steve, just get in there and pull,' Andy laughed. The stunt went off brilliantly and he looked rather good at the pre-show party, almost passable as woman.

The pre-show drinks party went on forever as the Spice Girls were running very late; later I found out it was also the night the girls split from Simon Fuller. During the long wait people were getting quite impatient and intoxicated. I was chatting to a friend when there was a tap on my shoulder and a very beautiful woman asked, 'Is there any food or canapés? I've brought my kids and this is going on forever.'

It was Paula Yates and she was completely out of it. I could not believe that she had the kids with her while she was in that state. Of course there was no food prior to the show. I asked her if she was OK, but of course she was not. 'Maybe I should go home,' she said, holding my hand. She was clearly hurting and lost. Much as I tried to get her something to eat, it was to no avail. I have no idea whether she did go home, but her face haunted me for some while – she looked so pained.

The show eventually went on and it was the only *An Audience With...* I'd seen where they had to do retakes. It was too dull to watch, so I spent more time looking back at hunky David Beckham, who sat alone in the audience.

There was just one problem with being a television hairdresser – it doesn't pay. There is an army of willing stylists happy to do it all for free in order to promote their shampoo line or salon. I had neither and, much as the kudos was welcome, it didn't pay my bills and I had hardly any time to do my existing clients. I was working 12 hours a day and promoting Sweeny's salon for free. It just wasn't sustainable. Not realising the other stylists were working for nothing, I invoiced GMTV. They did pay, but no more bookings to appear on the show came my way.

I wanted to be on the show once in a while, as it did have its advantages, so I quickly arranged to take Ben to lunch at Livebait. I explained the misunderstanding and said that, although I wouldn't be available to appear on a weekly basis, once a month for a name credit would be OK and he did use me again for a few spots. However, during a conversation months later at a lunch at my home with Ben and Liam Hamilton, it came up that my favourite show as a kid was *Bewitched*. I commented casually that it was great that it was back on television, adding that it cheered up my mornings. There was an awkward silence and, later, Liam pointed out my *faux pas* – *Bewitched* was on at the same time as Lorraine's show, Ben's baby, and it had been the worst thing I could have said. I'm not saying that sealed my fate, but no bookings for GMTV ever came through after that. Ben left a few months later and I sent my portfolio in to the woman who took his place. She had me in for a meeting and asked me to bring in some ideas for the show. She took the ideas and I saw a few of them put into play over the next few months, but she never booked me. Later on I bumped into her at the Hairdresser of the Year Awards sitting at the table of her hairdresser of choice, so that was that. It's all about who you know.

A year later, in July 1997, I was back at GMTV, not on screen but behind the scenes with the cast of *Baywatch*, who were in the UK to promote the show. Shelagh Pymm, a brilliant PR agent, had been asked by LWT to look after them during their stay and she hired me for the week to do their hair. It was an early start – 5am – and work often went on until 8pm; the money was not great, but it was good for my c.v. and I really liked Shelagh, having worked with her in the past.

The entire cast hadn't travelled over, but there was the man himself, David Hasselhoff, Donna D'Errico, Traci Bingham and David Chokachi. It was clear from the start that Traci and Donna were not best mates; neither came for their hair if the other was in the room and the only time they did was on photo shoots when it was impossible to do them separately.

Traci was lovely, kind and enthusiastic while Donna was curt, never overly friendly and a bit of a diva. The only time she turned into a sweet *Baywatch* babe was if David Hasselhoff was in the room. During one photo shoot I was styling her hair when she snarled: 'It's too much of a "do",' screwing her face up, making her look like a Pekinese. She went off and did the pictures and when David walked in and complimented her on her hair, she ran her hands through it and said: 'Oh, it's fab, David.' We all just looked at each other.

Traci loved her hair and I had a quiet word with Alan Strutt about doing a separate shoot with Traci. This resulted in Traci getting the front cover of *Maxim* magazine, Page Three of *The Sun* and a demand for shots of her from Stuart Higgins, *The Sun's* editor. LWT was thrilled, as was Traci. When Donna found out she snapped: 'How did she get that?' When she discovered I had arranged it she was lost for words, then quietly sat back and muttered, 'Oh, good for you,' screwing up her nose again Pekinese-style and glowering over at me.

The *Baywatch* girls look like they have been crafted out of the same mould; many have hair extensions, fake boobs, coloured contact lenses ... after a while they remind me of aliens. They can be disappointing in real life, but look good on television.

Mr Hasselhoff, unlike many stars, is tall, handsome and commanding and his PR person fussed over him like he was her ten-year-old son. She strictly instructed journalists that there was 'no smoking near Mr Hasselhoff', or 'Mr Hasselhoff is a vegetarian'. This was interesting as at the *This Morning* show I distinctly recollect him asking me to fetch him a full English breakfast. At the last night party, held at the celebrity hot spot Soho House, I was in the men's room with Mr Hasselhoff. 'Hey, Steve, you got a cigarette?' he asked and then happily puffed away.

At the farewell party Liam Hamilton bought David's PR a whip as a joke to help fend off journalists and the like. I think she needed to use it on 'the Hoff', not the journalists.

During the last day Traci could not thank me enough and

made a big show of asking for my address as she wanted to send me a thank you gift from Los Angeles. Everyone was very impressed but, having lived in LA, I knew different. I am still waiting for the present to arrive but, hey, that's showbiz!

10

Waiting for Gazza

'I accept that I am an alcoholic; that's the main thing. I think you've got to. But I try not to say that I'm an alcoholic. I prefer to say that it's a disease I've got.'

Paul Gascoigne

Just seconds away from the hustle and bustle of Notting Hill lay one of showbiz's best-kept secrets – the Lennox hotel. Kylie Minogue, Liz Hurley, Monica Lewinsky, Jamie and Louise Redknapp and Minnie Driver would often be seen wandering the corridors of what became one of London's hippest establishments. Footballer Paul Gascoigne took up residence there for a while and I also found myself living there one time when I was between apartments. It was so fabulous I never wanted to leave.

The Lennox hotel was run by a woman I like to call the Contessa Con Sharrock. Not because she ever conned anyone out of anything, but because she had the ability to get into any venue free and to ensure that she and her guests could drink all night without paying a penny. She was married to ex-soap heart-throb Ian Sharrock, who had left her penniless when he ran off to run a dog rescue centre in Tenerife.

Penniless or not, she holidayed in St Tropez, ate in all the best restaurants, kept her children in private schools and was on the list for all the best parties. If ever there was a truly unforgettable character, it was Pam Sharrock, the Contessa.

Pam was very popular among the showbiz crowd, many of whom used the hotel as a home from home. The Lennox was comfortable and relaxed and the Contessa, a brilliant hostess, made everyone feel part of the family.

On my first day there Pam rushed me straight to the bar, barely giving me time to unpack my things. She was desperate to introduce me to Brendan Cole, the heart-throb from *Strictly Come Dancing*. My nickname for him was the Splendid Mole but he had an extraordinary effect on women, who seemed to descend into giggling schoolgirls in his presence. When he spoke, they almost wet their knickers. Even the sophisticated Contessa changed when she was around him – a bomb could have dropped in the room and she'd still have been looking up adoringly at him, oblivious to anything around her.

There is a great shortage of good-looking straight men in London for women and, in an ideal world, women would marry their best gay friend and live happily ever after. Except for the sex, of course. Brendan was chic, charming, handsome and well groomed; in other words, the ultimate gay man, except for the fact that he was completely straight. He has a gay brother, whom I've met, and who's a lovely guy but he does not have Brendan's allure. I came up with the Splendid Mole nickname to wind up the women at the Lennox, because they talked about him all the time and they hated it when I got his name wrong.

Brendan had been hidden at the Lennox before going on *Celebrity Love Island*, and returned for another six weeks during *Strictly Come Dancing*. If Brendan ever wrote a kiss and tell book it would be one hell of a read, though I think he's too much of a gentleman to do that.

Pam also warned me that Paul Gascoigne was staying in the room next to the loyalty bar. She told me to be careful of him; he was a lovely man, she said, but a little indiscreet about some of his friends. Paul had been staying there for the past few months and the Contessa was a great friend of his, and his manager at the time, Jane Morgan. Paul's stepdaughter, the model Bianca, had appeared on *Celebrity Love Island* with Brendan but his behaviour towards her had not gone down well with Paul and he had taken a dislike to Brendan (though they later made up).

During my first few days at the Lennox I didn't see the famous footballer at all, mainly due the fact that we kept different hours; he stayed up late and never seemed to surface before midday while I am an early bird. The thought of meeting him filled me with dread, if I'm honest.

One afternoon I popped into the bar to get a Coke to take to my room and I noticed the Contessa chatting to a group of people, including Paul. He was sitting at the centre of the group sipping on a whisky, with two mobile phones, his cigarettes and lighter laid out neatly on the table in front of him.

The Contessa waved me over but, as I didn't really want to be introduced, I signalled that I was going upstairs. Before I could, though, Paul shouted out: 'Hey, Shane Warne, who the hell are you?' He thought I looked like the Australian cricketer and Pam explained that I was the friend she had told him about. He took a long look at me, then he said, 'I am nay gay but he is a good-looking fella.' He almost choked on his whisky when I replied, 'Ta, I am gay though, and you don't look bad yourself, mate.' Paul then insisted that I had a drink. We sat chatting for a bit and I found him fascinating. I had never met anyone so damaged, so vulnerable and so self-obsessed. In the end I stayed talking to him the whole evening.

The root of Gazza's problem seemed to be the lack of affection and approval from his father who, according to Paul, had never seen a single one of his games. I met his old man only once and even the air around him felt cold. He looked a lot like the comedian Dick Emery and wore way too much jewellery (mostly presents from Gazza).

Paul, though not that big, is tough – I saw him put his hand through a wall once – but he was terrified of his father. His dad hit him only once, though he knocked him over a sofa in the process. Paul's problem was that he could never do enough to get his father's approval, no matter how many cars or how much jewellery was lavished on him.

At the time I was working for one of my clients, travelling with her, doing her hair and organising her bookings. She did not need me for a few weeks so I had some time on my hands. Paul suggested I did his hair the next day, and I said that I would. When you are freelancing, going to people's homes, offices or hotels, it's best to set definite ground rules, otherwise you will find that some can really take advantage. You might arrive to find them having a long soak in the bath, or in a meeting or taking a 20-minute phone call. Charge them by the hour, or a half-day rate, and always insist on a full day's notice of cancellation. Many people seem to think it's OK to just cancel their hairdresser at a moment's notice but are far more careful with, say, their dentist, who would insist on a cancellation fee if 24 hours notice isn't given.

Well, needless to say, Paul did not turn up to have his hair done the next morning. It seemed he had got up in time but that over breakfast he'd read an article in *The Sun* that really upset him. What could be worse than appearing in *I'm a Celebrity ... Get Me Out of Here?* the article asked. Answer: 'Waking up one morning to discover that you're Gazza.' He was so upset he went straight back to his room.

Paul had the papers delivered to his room religiously every morning. Pam and I took to checking them before they were delivered; if there were any slighting references to him, we simply told him they had not arrived. He also hated seeing sexy pictures

130

of Bianca in the paper so we also hid the ones in which she appeared. I did suggest that he stopped reading the tabloids, as many other celebrities have, but to no avail. He was still obsessing about the piece when I met with him later.

'Can you believe this, man?' he said, shoving the paper in my face. Then he started drinking, as he always did when he was upset about something.

Paul had support – Robbie Williams would text and David Beckham rang numerous times to make sure he was OK. Paul would also ring his mum but his language towards her was indecent at times. He asked to speak to my mother once when she rang me, as I had chatted to his mum. On that occasion he had said to his mother, 'Speak to this lovely guy, man, he's gay but I love him.' Much as my mum might have liked to speak to the great Gazza, the thought of the language he might use was too much for me, and I refused.

Paul was losing weight and looked so ill. He promised me he was eating properly but I began to have my doubts. Apart from the Haribo sweets packets, which he had laid out neatly by the half dozen in his bedroom drawer, there was other evidence. I always bought my breakfast from outside the hotel and started bringing him something too: a bagel with cheese, turkey and avocado, which he would eat half of to keep me happy and hide the rest away. He loved Nando's, and would actually eat a whole meal from there. I discovered that while I was away working in Lapland for a few days, he had shoved a baseball cap on his head and gone out to get one for himself.

I suggested that Paul have his hair done in the afternoon. He's a pretty well-groomed fellow anyway – he has had botox, eyelash tints and facials. Going out, he would wear mascara and blusher; in fact, he would have made a good WAG! But suggesting the afternoon was also a bad idea. He was still feeling bad and wanted to have a chat – and a wee toddy. The Contessa would make these for him and he really liked her fussing around him in a motherly fashion. But, predictably, the chat turned into an all-day bender and the hair was forgotten about again.

During my time hanging out with Paul, a number of what he called 'fruitcakes' would regularly turn up at the hotel. These girls claimed to be concerned for Paul's welfare but were only really interested in his celebrity status. Rather than rushing off to bed with them, Paul preferred to stay and chat with us, and seemed exasperated by them. They always wanted something. I remember one girl asking him, at around nine o'clock one evening, whether he would ring a producer he knew at Sky TV about a presenting job for her. I was pleased when Jimmy Five Bellies, who was visiting at the time, told her to sling her hook. Another, who was a psychiatric nurse, hung around all the time even though Paul was really rude to her. She must have been suffering from low self-esteem; in the entire three months I was there, I only saw Paul take her up to his room once. I think he liked the company of men better.

Sheryl, Paul's ex-wife, went public on Paul's violence towards her but she continued to call him and kept his name, as did Bianca. Paul hated it when Bianca called him Paul – 'Call me Dad,' he would say.

I only saw Paul be violent once, when he put his hand through a wall in the Lennox after a night out, damaging not only the wall but his hand too. The owners of the hotel wanted Paul out, not just because of the damage, but because he could be so rude to the other guests.

On one occasion Paul greeted a slightly overweight man with the comment: 'Black isn't always slimming, mate.' He would ask people to move if they were taking 'his' space in the bar. I think it was more due to his OCD than complete rudeness. If strangers came into the room he would often just walk out or ask those he was drinking with to come up to his room instead. He also had a habit of showing the two tattoos on his waist that he'd had done in Mexico after a few drinks. That wasn't too bad – but then the cock would come out too; just 'for a laugh'.

One day I was chatting to an American literary agent who was visiting the hotel, but, after about ten minutes, she asked if our chat was upsetting my 'partner'. I looked around and Paul had a face like thunder, demanding that I come and sit with him. She was surprised when I replied: 'No, he's a mate and he is straight.'

Luckily the Contessa was very fond of Paul, as we all were, and told Jamie Bloom, the owner, that she would raise Paul's room rate instead and have me keep an eye on him. Being the Contessa, who could persuade anyone of anything, Jamie agreed.

Paul did not want his hand injury hitting the papers, so he refused to go out to see a doctor. However, after three days he was in such pain, and his method of treating the injury – drinking lots – was clearly not working. It was also making him unbearable. So I called a private doctor to come out to him at the hotel early in the morning. The doctor was a nice enough sort but I think he was taken aback when his unnamed patient turned out to be Gazza – and a stark naked Gazza at that.

When I suggested to Paul that he might like me to help him put some shorts on, he replied: 'Nay, I am all right, man, he's seen it all before.' Francesco, a handsome young man who worked at the hotel, arrived in the room with some tea for Paul at the same time. The doctor looked at me, then at the naked Gazza, and the stunning Francesco, and enquired: 'What kind of hotel is this?'

The prognosis was not good – if Paul did not get his hand sorted out, he could lose the use of it altogether and he needed to see a specialist. Paul was ready to settle in for another day of drinking but I am used to dealing with difficult divas and I had him dressed and on the way to Harley Street in double-quick time.

Paul seemed to find it all very amusing – he became boyish and pliant and I think it was the fact that someone cared for him. On the way to Harley Street I got a taste of what it was like for him to be constantly in the public eye. When I'm out with soap stars, people don't usually bat an eye but with Paul every other person stopped and said hello.

The next day he bought me some beautiful cufflinks as a thank you. Paul is an extremely generous man and often used to tip the staff huge amounts, or buy presents for everyone. I think that in a way he was trying to buy their love, as he did with his family. The Contessa asked the staff just to take what was reasonable and give the rest back – and they did. That's the beauty of being in a small hotel and he was much more protected there than he would have been in a larger, more impersonal establishment.

Paul started to behave himself, staying in and drinking less. I saw him off to bed one night and went to sleep myself. But next morning he was nowhere to be seen and Francesco told me that ten minutes after I went to bed, Paul sneaked out of his room and left the hotel. We soon discovered he was in police custody after getting into a fight with a photographer outside Prince Harry's haunt, Boujis.

Apparently one of the 'fruitcakes' had called him up and begged him to meet her there. It turned out she just wanted to get her picture in the paper and knew that being with Paul would do the trick. Paul never refused an autograph or a picture and said that he had stopped and said a snap could be taken, but that the photographer had chased him and shoved him with the camera, so he had just lashed out.

Pam went to pick Paul up from the police station but by now the paparazzi had found his secret hideaway. So the link between

Paul and the Lennox was uncovered and, before long, the Contessa would find she had to check any new bookings at the hotel to see whether they were by undercover tabloid journalists. On several occasions, though, they slipped through the net. Paul moved to the Hilton for a few days in an effort to throw them off the scent, slipping back to the Lennox late at night.

Paul's great friend, Jimmy, is a man I can only describe as an enabler; in other words, he enables Paul to behave destructively and does little to protect his friend from himself. I did see Jimmy stick up for Paul on a few occasions, mainly if he thought someone was taking the piss or getting in the way of him being at the centre of attention with Paul. However, I felt he did little to curb Paul's addictions and when Jimmy was around all hell broke loose. He nicknamed me Christmas Steve, and I think he was a little jealous of Paul's relationship with me. He knew better than to attempt to shove me out of the way, however, and decided to be friendly instead. In fact, he rang me from Newcastle when he took Paul home for a visit and wanted me to jump on a train and join them. I politely declined as partying with them, particularly away from my home territory, sounded like a bad idea.

By the time he got back, I had moved into my new flat. Paul came over for drinks with Francesco and a girl called Mila, who worked in the office at the hotel. When I brought out canapés, he was beside himself. 'I knew it, man. I knew if I came here you would have canapés.'

Almost three months after I first suggested it, I finally got to do Paul's hair. I told him that *The Sun* had once sent me to paint the red St George's cross on his head but that I had spent all day sitting in a field outside the England team's training camp with reporter Dawn Neesom (now editor of the *Daily Star*). Luckily Dawn had an amazing dry sense of humour so I didn't get bored. As darkness fell, we realised it wasn't going to happen and took off to the pub. Paul loved the way I did his hair and would always call me on the phone or text me when someone complimented him on it.

I was doing some work for a client in Malta with a wonderful hotel called the Fortina. Paul needed a break and so it was arranged he would travel to Malta with his father, John, as a guest of the Fortina. Paul is a demigod on the island, which is predominantly Catholic, and for Maltese football fans there is God and then there's Gazza – and not necessarily in that order.

My client, for whom I was working exclusively, had become increasingly erratic and obsessive. She would send strange texts to me, telling me to get hypnosis, and when I went to her room to blow-dry her hair, I'd sometimes find her naked. It all became quite stressful. She travelled to Malta a great deal and on one occasion she kept me waiting at Gatwick airport for four and a half hours, refusing to answer her phone. When she did arrive, there were no apologies; she'd rebooked the flight out of Heathrow. It was a nightmare and after we parted company she harassed me so much I was forced to file a complaint at Notting Hill police station. She had seemed so nice at first but when I suggested we had a contract, she wouldn't hear of it. My advice is never to take a job looking after just one person, or travelling abroad without a proper contract. My nightmare client moved the goalposts and treated me appallingly when I would not play ball.

The end result of this was that I was advised to stay away from Malta for a bit as she had powerful friends over there. I took Paul to the airport but he became nervous when I said I was not going, as he hates flying. He said he wanted to cancel the trip if I was not going but we managed to persuade him to board the flight. Once on board, he started to drink heavily to calm his nerves. Paul arrived drunk in Malta. Cliff Anguis, one of the hotel managers, called me up from the car on the way from the airport and I could hear how off the wall Paul was. It was a sign of what was to come on the unsupervised trip.

The Fortina was always happy to have celebrities staying as the other guests liked it and it was good for publicity. Initially, the presence of Paul's ice-cold father was a calming influence on him, and he'd send his son to bed if he got too much. But Paul hooked up with Calum Best (son of British football legend, George Best) who was also staying at the hotel, and it wasn't long before Paul was on the phone at one in the morning asking whether I knew anyone who could get him some party favours on the island.

Paul's manager, Jane Morgan, was less than pleased that I had not gone on the trip, especially when a statement from Malta by Gazza – apparently released by his agent – appeared on the Internet. Jane was polite, as always, when she asked me if I was Paul's manager now as well as his hairdresser. She listened quietly as I explained it was Jimmy who had been speaking for Paul. 'That makes sense,' she replied, and apologised for calling so late.

Paul started to claim that the hotel was booking personal appearances for him, but this turned out not to be true. He had agreed to one interview while out drinking, when he bumped into someone from the local station. He agreed to some filming in a local bar down the road from the hotel. It was arranged by a good friend of mine on the island, Michael Gatt, who arranged that Paul was paid in cash. But Paul, wanting to please everyone, agreed to all the other requests too and was soon begging me to tell them to leave him alone.

Paul was getting people I knew on the island to run errands and to pick up party favours. One night my phone rang at two in the morning – it was a good mate who is a bit of a star in Malta. I had arranged for him to have dinner with Paul, whom he idolised, and I thought it would be good for Paul to meet him too. My friend was initially happy to run errands for Paul, who started calling him wanting party favours. The errand had been run but Paul could not be found. 'What should I do?' my friend asked me, though it was the middle of the night and I was hundreds of miles away in London. Truly, I wanted to tell him to tell Mr Gascoigne to fuck off but instead I spent hours tracking Paul down and reunited him with his latest errand boy.

Needless to say, it was a relief when Paul came home. He likes to dominate the men in his life that he feels are looking after him and, though he is not gay, he does have 'man crushes'. I think this stems from the lack of affection and security from his father when he was growing up. Pretty soon he stopped calling me and I was replaced by a personal trainer, an ex-SAS man called Dylan. He would tell Paul what to do and instruct others how they should handle the former footballer. Dylan even had the nerve to tell the Contessa what to do with Paul and was keen to get him out of the Lennox. The Contessa put him straight on that one, though after an incident with another guest, she finally had no choice but to ask Dylan to leave. Paul stayed on to the bitter end of the hotel's life; it is now a block of upmarket apartments.

In Paul's world, an SAS officer making him stay clean and get fit was a pipe dream but, as with all crushes, it didn't last. It was not long before I opened the paper and there he was, back with Jimmy and falling out of a train drunk in Newcastle.

Late one night the phone rang and it was Paul, who had just got out of rehab. He wanted me to come over and party with him and a fruitcake girl. I said no but promised to do his hair the day after. Then Jimmy rang and asked me to do some favours for him to help sort out Paul. None of the favours sounded as though they would be good for Paul in the long run – and I don't do those kind of favours for anyone. Much as I liked Paul a lot, partying with him would in the end have made me just another enabler.

The next day I changed my number and have not seen him since. I do hope he gets better, but I fear there is not enough love in the world to give poor Paul the peace and security he so desperately craves.

11

The Madness of Celebrity

While I was living in the States, one day I was due to fly from LA to New York on the Friday red-eye, aptly named as it takes all night to get there (though you can avoid the red eyes if you bring along your blue eyedrops and Elizabeth Arden eight-hour cream; the supermodels never fly without them). The job was to fly in and colour and blow-dry a client's hair. Quite by chance, Lester Middlehurst called to say he was also flying to New York, to interview the Yorkshire-born author, Barbara Taylor Bradford. He was seeing her at her New York apartment and wanted to stay in LA with me afterwards.

He was even more thrilled when he heard I was bound for the Big Apple too. The client had called a few days earlier, begging me to make the 5,000-mile return trip to New York just to do her hair. 'Nobody blow-dries like you, darling, please, please say you'll come,' she urged. As she also promised first-class travel, hotel bills for two nights and a reasonable fee, I thought, why not? It would also free me up for an evening with Lester when we could catch up on news and paint the town red. So I moved my other clients around and boarded the red-eye flight.

The last time we'd met in New York, we had gone to see *Grapes of Wrath* on Broadway and had sat behind Roseanne Barr and her then husband, Tom Arnold, who were flying to London by Concorde the next day on their honeymoon. Hearing our accents, Tom turned round and asked us about where to go in

London and later we went backstage to meet the cast. Roseanne spent ages chatting to the youngsters in the cast about school and came over as a genuinely nice person. We got on well with them until they discovered, via the PR person, that Lester was a famous London journalist. Then they didn't seem so keen, probably because Roseanne had been having some bad press in the States. They declined Lester's offer to come for a drink but did thank us for all our tips. Or perhaps they just wanted to be alone on their honeymoon.

Lester begged me to come to his hotel as soon as I arrived in New York so we could have breakfast and, in true Lester style, when I arrived he was in bed with a one-night stand he'd met in The Eagle bar the night before.

The next piece of news was that Barbara Taylor Bradford and her husband, the television producer Robert Bradford, had invited Lester to their home for dinner, so he wasn't free for the evening after all. He said we could go out after the dinner but, knowing him as I did, and what he was like around celebrities, the weekend was looking like a bit of a washout.

I checked into the Paramount hotel and grabbed a late breakfast in the Village with Lester, who was full of chat about the hot man that had just left his hotel bedroom. Sipping a milky coffee and playing with a runny omelette, Lester suddenly came up with the idea of simply asking the Bradfords if he could bring an old friend to dinner, one he'd just run into in New York. Why he just couldn't tell them that he'd already arranged to have dinner with me I don't know, but perhaps that would have been too simple for Lester. Anyway he was sure that they would let me come and I went off to do my client.

Lester called later, thrilled to bits, to say that I was indeed welcome to come to dinner at the Bradfords. I dashed out and picked up a gift for Barbara, a book of Beryl Cook prints. An hour later Lester picked me up, very excited about the evening ahead. Not happy with telling Barbara the story of bumping into a long lost friend, he had added that I was an old school pal. Lester was eight years my senior and, with his moustache, looked much older than me. I didn't like him making stuff up but it was too late to do anything about it and we dashed off to Manhattan.

Barbara and her husband could not have been lovelier, though when I gave her my gift she opened it, put it down and politely thanked me. She did not seem that pleased with it and I was a bit embarrassed and wished I'd brought flowers instead. They lived in the most opulent New York apartment but Barbara was really down to earth and had great northern charm. She had three other guests, including two women friends from England. Over dinner one of them asked Lester how he knew me, and Lester replied that we'd gone to school together, moving on swiftly in an attempt to change the subject. No such luck – the two women were friends from Barbara's school days and wanted to talk more about it. One of them said we did not look the same age. 'No, we're not,' I replied. 'I was Lester's fag.' Lester almost spat his drink out but enough alcohol had been consumed to let us get away with it and it was a terrific evening. Later I gave Barbara a hand with the dishes and she even pinched my bottom in the kitchen. She was a hoot.

Next day she rang us and asked to speak to me, and apologised for not noticing how lovely the book of illustrations was. It was a great weekend. But I did wonder why Lester had to make up a story about going to school together when he could just have said, 'My best mate is in town, can I bring him please?' But he was always like that when celebrities were involved.

You can never tell these days who is going to be catapulted to the dizzy heights of stardom. Once it used to be that if you were a performer, after years of training and treading the boards with rep companies in tiny venues up and down the country you might just get a lucky break. You would work long and hard and really earn your chance of fame. Now, with reality show contestants, supermodels and even tabloid journalists becoming household names almost overnight, you can never tell who will be the next big thing. One thing's for sure, when fame comes it changes lives for ever.

Who would have guessed that a talentless, teenage Jordan, who rubbed many up the wrong way, would become an international star, with a feeding frenzy of paparazzi wherever she goes? Or that Jade Goody, the late *Big Brother* star, would spend most of her short adult life in front of the TV cameras without having a single discernible talent? For good or bad, she captured the nation's attention.

I have never done more than shake hands with Piers Morgan at parties or events, but it has been fascinating to watch his meteoric rise. Though Piers is a genuinely talented journalist, he has always reminded me of the school bully, and at parties he loved to go up to celebrities he'd just exposed to rub salt into the wounds. My first meeting with him was at the opening night of Victoria Wood's show at the Albert Hall. I was chatting away to Dale Winton, who had been outed by Piers' paper, *The Mirror*, for having had colonic irrigation at the clinic next to Sweeny's salon. Piers immediately rushed up to Dale, with a smirk on his face. 'How's the bottom, Dale, eh?' he asked, giggling like a schoolboy. Dale took it in good spirit, but seemed pleased when Piers moved on.

He did the same thing at Jane Moore and Gary Farrow's wedding reception. I had done Jane's hair the day before and Gary Cockerill had waved his magic wand and done the bride's make-up at Elton John's home on the day, a gift from Barbara Windsor. It could not have been more of a fairy-tale day; the location was the stunning ballroom of Claridge's hotel, which was full of big showbiz names. Jane and Gary's friend of many years, Elton John, was going to perform and it was all very impressive. Jane was not in the least bit celebrity-struck but did coin the great line: 'I am the only person in the room I've never heard of before.'

As with all fairy-tales there has to be a villain and, for once, it was not John Lesley, who looked dashing in his dress kilt. It was Piers Morgan, the school bully, who sneaked up behind Anthea Turner and her partner, Grant Bovey, and whispered a little dig about something or other that had been in the paper. 'Ah, Piers, you must be enjoying all the love and warmth directed to you in the room,' said Anthea sarcastically, before turning back to continue her chat with me. That was the second time I'd met Piers and it certainly didn't change my opinion of him.

Later at the sit-down dinner it was so great to be with Barbara Windsor and her husband Scott Mitchell; Nick Faldo sat on the same table and we were joined by Piers. I was pleased as I wanted to get to know more about the man who had become the youngest editor in Fleet Street history. Then Sue Brealey, the former head of press for GMTV, took her place at the table and things started to unravel. A row erupted between Piers and Sue over something Piers had written or allowed to appear about Mr Motivator, the former exercise guru on GMTV. Piers would not leave it alone and was really enjoying getting a rise out of Sue. There was a brief truce at one point, as the best man, Elton John, sang to the happy couple. In the end, though, I had to suggest that Sue moved, which calmed things down for a while. But soon Piers was making comments across the table at her and wouldn't let it go. So, although he was, by all accounts an amazing editor and a hard worker, that vital ingredient of charm appeared to be lacking and he seemed to get off on getting a rise out of people.

When Piers started his television show, *Tabloid Tales*, interviewing celebrities he had often exposed in the past, it was a little like a serial killer returning to scene of the crime. But the same celebrities who would sneer when he came into a room still rushed to be interviewed by him – showbiz people have short memory spans when publicity is involved.

A very dear friend of mine was in hospital and we feared she did not have long to live. People had visited from all over, and she had bravely greeted them and joined in the banter even though she could barely lift her head without assistance. The hospital had never seen so many well-wishers and had to restrict the numbers visiting in the end. Though friends travelled from as far away as the States, I was shocked at her reaction to one phone call. It was the entertainer Bruce Forsyth, who wasn't a close friend of hers. But the excitement of a celebrity calling injected new life into the invalid; she practically leaped up from the bed when she heard he was planning to visit, shoving the phone at me with the order: ' Give Bruce really good directions!' Well, I'd give Bruce the same directions as I'd given anyone else; there is no special celebrity version of how to get from A to B.

My immediate thought was that surely his driver could find his way to a well-known London hospital, with or without a sat nav. But I had to tell him three times where the hospital was and could not wait to get him off the phone. As I left the hospital later, I thought how I and many other close friends had visited every day and run around getting things, and doing her hair, but had never been given such a greeting. If I were on my way out, I know I'd prefer to have my real friends around me – the last thing I'd want would be someone I barely knew seeing me at my worst, and saying, 'Nice to see you, to see you nice.'

While many celebrities live in an unreal world, there are plenty of others who are down to earth. Often, the people who represent them are worse and members of the public can behave really badly when it comes to stars. They seem to feel that, because they recognise a public figure, they have some sort of rights over them.

Anthea Turner had a tricky incident with a fan at the Formula 1 ball, which was held in the beautiful grounds of Stowe School in Buckinghamshire. She was enjoying an after-dinner drink with Jane Moore, Emma Noble and me, and we were waiting for the firework show to start. Anthea had met an admirer at the dinner and had signed an autograph for him and chatted a bit. But the man just would not leave her alone. Anthea explained that she was enjoying an evening with close friends, and would like to be left alone now. He took no notice and Jane and Anthea asked me to get him to leave (really, they thought that I was that butch!).

So I explained that we were just a group of close friends trying to have some quality time together. 'Yeah, yeah,' said the man, who had obviously had a couple too many vodka and Red Bulls (Red Bull were sponsoring the event), and he continued to pester Anthea. Putting it bluntly, I told him it was time to leave, at which point he turned nasty and threatened to 'take me out'. I realised that he had probably watched Anthea on *Blue Peter* as a boy and that meeting her was a boyhood fantasy. In the end, I asked how he would feel if he was out with his mates and someone, no matter how charming, kept bursting in on it. His face turned to thunder and I was sure I was a goner, but instead he looked at Anthea for a moment, turned and stroked my jacket lapel and said: 'You've got a point, mate. No hard feelings eh?' and walked away.

On another occasion I was sitting in a corner at the Café Royal with Anna Ryder Richardson, enjoying a drink and discussing a project. An autograph hunter came over, full of smiles. 'Sorry to interrupt but would you mind?' she said, and shoved a piece of paper towards Anna. Miss Ryder is always charming and happy to take time for a fan but this woman sat down to talk and, despite many hints, was still there 15 minutes later. Bar saying 'LOVE, FUCK OFF!' there seemed to be no way to get rid of her, so we just got up and went somewhere else.

When you're working with celebrities you need to be ready for anything. Once I was booked to style two red wigs for Emma Noble and Melinda Messenger, who were going to get into bed with one of Britain's most famous redheads, Chris Evans, as part of a sketch for his *TFI Friday* show. The girls were to turn red in the bed, wearing their red wigs. I asked whether this meant that Chris would be going blond and should I pick up a blond wig? I was told that Chris would not be going blond but instinct made me pick up an extra wig for him so I could have it just in case.

When we got to Riverside Studio, where they filmed the show, we had to wait for Chris who was rehearsing. He was telling off one of the actors, coming down really hard on him and I was glad it wasn't me. When he eventually got round to us, though, he was lovely and full of energy. We filmed him with the girls in bed, blonde, and then when I got the girls into their red wigs, Chris suddenly shouted: 'Where's my blond wig?' There was a stunned silence. Then I pulled the blond wig out of my bag, saying, 'Here you go, Chris.' When I jumped onto the bed and shoved it on his head, he was a little speechless. I'm not sure what it was all about but I have a feeling if I hadn't thought to bring the wig along, despite having been told not to, it would all have been my fault.

Equally, when on a work trip with *Emmerdale* star Nicola Wheeler to the Dominican Republic, we ran into one of those 'celebrity deniers'. These are people who think it's cool to pretend not to know who a celebrity is when of course they do. It can be very irritating. Nicola and I were having dinner with a friend who was looking after us for the holiday company that was sponsoring our trip when we were joined by another rep. Almost before she sat down, she asked if she was supposed to know who Nicola was.

Now you won't find a less starry, down-to-earth actress than Nicola Wheeler. Brought up on a council estate, she has worked since she was 14, and what you see is what you get. She smiled and said politely, 'No, love,' and introduced herself. 'No, you are in something,' the rep persisted. '*Emmerdale*,' Nicola replied, and continued to sip her margarita.

'Oh, I don't watch soaps, me,' the woman said as she looked at her menu. That was good, as it was the last thing Nicola or I wanted to talk about. But no sooner had we ordered our food than the rep carried on: 'Mind you my aunty does, so I see it at hers when I visit. But I don't pay attention, to be honest.' She then spent the next two hours talking about every detail of *Emmerdale* and the other soaps. Nicola and I were kicking ourselves under the table; obviously she was a huge fan but, instead of being honest, she lied, trying to be cool, though the truth is it made her look the complete opposite.

Nicola has always been fun, from the very first time we met. I had travelled to the little town of Colne in Lancashire for a feature called 'Back to My First Job', where I would take stars back to where they had first worked. Nicola was the first celebrity to feature in the series. The town was steeped in thick fog when I got there and my hotel was a little way out. When I looked out of my window, it looked like the setting for *An American Werewolf in London*.

I set off to meet Nicola at the Italian restaurant in which she used to work. It was called Carlo's and run by Carlo and his lovely wife, Lesley. The waitress clothes that I needed for the shoot had been sent to me, as I had not had time to pick them out. To my horror, when I got them out, they had sent me an outfit more suited to a 1920s Agatha Christie-style teashop.

Nicola arrived and seemed really sweet; she had brought along her boyfriend, Jason Waller, who looked a very posh playboy type. I gave her the clothes (without the hat and Rosa Klebb shoes) and she went to change. A minute later she was back, with a look of horror on her face. 'I am not wearing this,' she said, but was full of apologies and assured me that she was not just being difficult. I could see the problem: the skirt came down near her ankles and she looked awful in it. Luckily for me, Carlo had a short black skirt and white shirt for Nicola to wear. I think she was wondering what the hell my game was. I kept telling her I had not done the clothes and had had them sent via a stylist who I had borrowed them from Angels, an amazing costume shop.

After the shoot I stayed on and had one of the nicest Italian meals with Nicola and Jason, the posh boyfriend who turned out to be far from a playboy and was hysterically funny. Nicola was the one in charge in the relationship and she was a far cry from the type of actress/model who goes out with flash men. The two lived in a small flat near Marylebone with their hamster, Crumble.

Liking the couple so much, I set up a holiday trip to Jamaica at Sandals for them and covered it for the *News of the World* magazine. It was a great holiday and though Nicola and Jason wanted me to stay I only went for four days to sort pictures. But the pictures were truly dreadful. I had used a great photographer so I'm not sure what happened, but Jason looked like a wet blanket in several of them, and he's a good-looking fella. But they saw the funny side and, as long as I went with a different photographer, Nicola agreed to do more work with me. However, the two split up a month later and Nicola jokes that it was the curse of Steven.

When negotiating to take celebrities on trips, their agents can insist on first-class travel, the choice of what their clients will wear and will often demand picture/copy approval. But you should always be careful what you agree to, as it can be a nightmare getting pictures and words past agents even if they're really complimentary about their clients. Often agents do it as a way of justifying their existence – and their fees – though the top ones are usually professional about these things.

Two years later Nicola agreed to walk the Inca Trail in Peru to raise awareness for the Alzheimer's Society. I was covering it for *Hello Magazine*, who love their pictures glossy and glamorous. Nicola's gran had passed away with the illness so Nicola was keen to help. There were no demands, except that we shared a tent on the five-day hike, as she did not want to share with a stranger.

It was a long flight via Houston with a connecting flight to the capital of Peru, Lima, and we stayed in a hotel there for five hours. Jamie Hughes, the trip photographer, shared a room with Nicola and me. When I say a hotel, it was more like a prison, as there were so many bars on the windows. As the front door banged behind us and was locked, it dawned on us that Lima might not be as safe as one would like. Nicola took it all in her stride, including sharing a room with Jamie and me. We all laughed so hard and hardly got any sleep before taking off back to the airport to catch the one-hour flight to the town of Cusco, and then our base camp for the Inca Trail.

We were warned not to drink the night before taking the trail because of possible altitude sickness, as Cusco was 3,360m above sea level. This did not stop Nicola and me downing a couple of the local pisco sours at the local casino, and we woke with a little party hangover. After all, we had been presented with a flattened guinea pig as our first course (a delicacy in Peru) and we needed a drink.

Many of the fellow charity walkers seemed a lot older, and we felt confident that we'd find the hike a lot easier than they would. But never judge a book by its cover – some were yoga experts and we had no idea how fit they were. We had a shock when we got started – I had been so confident it was going to be an amble that I nearly refused hiking sticks, but thank God I agreed to take them anyway as I needed them.

I had never camped before and was truly dreading our first night. The noise of wild dogs and snoring from the other tents was doing nothing to lull me to sleep. Nicola and I were giggling like two schoolgirls and it was hard to get to sleep even though we were exhausted with the walking. She asked me to come with her to the toilet and I agreed, even though it was a bit of a hike in the pitch dark with just a torch to guide us. You could smell the toilets well before you got there though. As we only had one torch Nicola took it and I waited outside, jumping every time I heard a strange noise or a dog barked. 'This reminds me of when I was a kid camping,' Nicola said, wiping her hand with a wet wipe. Not wanting to be a spoilsport I just nodded. Then she piped up: 'I fucking hated it!'

Next day we woke to the sound of water wooshing against our tent. It was Jamie Hughes who thought he'd wake us up by urinating over the back of our tent. We could have happily killed him, but there was no time for that; it was on with the hike. It was certainly not as easy as it looked, though Nicola seemed to skip the miles, she was so agile. The scenery was breathtaking, though a large dead tarantula gave us a quick reminder that there were hidden dangers en route.

After two days we took to camping though, and were having a blast. Buying booze in the evening from locals and partying till late Nicola and I would fall into the tent to sleep. Nicola nicknamed me her tent bitch, as though we were in prison.

Hello likes its pictures to look polished but we had not showered or washed our hair for three days and looked far from glamorous to say the least. Luckily Nicola does not need much make-up to look good, though her hair was definitely not at its best. So we decided to use head scarves and it worked; she looked good. On other shoots it was just us and the crew, but here we could not hold up our fellow walkers so could not spend ages setting up pretty pictures. That's why I would only take a photographer or celebrity I know well on something like this. Jamie was a pro and snapped as he walked. Nicola was quick during the breaks to get in position for the right picture.

Five days later we had a great set of pictures, which appeared over five pages in *Hello*. Nicola was a trooper and never moaned once, and was at the front of every activity. She appeared on *This Morning* to talk about her experience and still champions the charity.

Taking celebrities away *en masse* can be very hard work. Whilst away on a trip to Malta, staying at the Fortina spa hotel for a Mother's Day special with Denise Welch and her lovely mother, Annie, I suggested that Denise had her 49th birthday over there in May, and I would cover it for *OK Magazine*.

The Fortina marketing team courted publicity and loved to have celebrities stay there. They said they would cover the flights and all-inclusive accommodation, with two complimentary treatments per day. In return, the hotel would get pictures of the celebrities and I would place an article in a UK paper or magazine.

Denise loved the idea, and came up with a list of other celebrities who could join the celebrations. They were Angela Lonsdale, an old friend of Denise's who played Emma Taylor in *Coronation Street*; Tricia Penrose, star of *Heartbeat*; singer Dee C Lee (Paul Weller's ex-wife); and *Dancing on Ice* winner and actress, Gaynor Faye.

That is where I should have left the list, just adding my own name and that of a make-up artist and stylist, but I thought that, as it was a birthday party, why not get Debbie, Denise's sister and an excellent make-up artist, to come along and bring Denise's close friend, Rose Hirst, to do the clothes. Denise loved the idea.

The hotel provided accommodation for hairdresser, make-up

artist and stylist but they were flown over economy, and had a basic spa room, which was perfectly fine for most people who came to assist me. The stars came over business class on Air Malta and stayed in deluxe spa rooms with their own private pool.

I spoke to Debbie in Newcastle and she was delighted. I explained to Rose that, as the girls would be wearing their own clothes, it was an easy shout for her, particularly with her theatre background.

Organising the flight with the hectic schedules of the stars was, of course, a nightmare. Some were OK to fly from Heathrow, but others wanted Manchester or Newcastle, and they could not all fly on the same day. Rose Hirst helped me get the actresses working up north sorted on the flights.

Then there were the treatments. The spa wanted them all booked in advance as they were getting full up. So I spent a day booking them all in for various luxury spa treatments. It took hours on the phone and e-mailing but I managed it. I realised that I had some left over, so booked them in and circled them in red. I e-mailed Rose saying that although the hotel would not give complimentary treatments for my crew, she should go down and enjoy herself and, if asked, to just say that Denise had asked her to go instead.

It was a relief when I got it all done and I was feeling rather pleased with myself, until Denise said that Rose didn't want to go now as she felt she was getting 'crumbs off the celebrity table'. For once, I was speechless. I had gone out of my way to make the trip as nice as possible for Rose, and had explained from the start that both she and Debbie were coming as my crew, so would not get celebrity status.

It seemed that somewhere along the line there had been some confusion, so I found myself on the phone apologising for something I had not done! I had to ring one of the hotel managers,

Cliff Agius, to say the trip was off unless Rose got the treatments in her name.

Debbie was no problem though, and was thrilled when she got to the hotel and couldn't wait to do the make-up and styling. But then we had another problem. Denise, who was not drinking at the time, said all the treatment times were too early in the day and she wanted them all changed. The problem with working with a very dear friend like Denise is that she sees me like a brother and can on occasions take advantage. She was so excited about all her friends being there that, unusually for her, she was being a diva. Putting my foot down, I told her they were busy and the treatments could not be changed.

Mike, the owner of the hotel, joined us at breakfast and asked if Denise was happy. She said how great it all was but then, in a little girl voice, she squeaked: 'All our treatments are booked too early in the day and we want to sunbathe.' Mike said it was no problem: 'Give Steven the times you want and we can sort it.' Debbie had worked as a beautician and knew how disruptive changing the treatments would be and snapped at Denise. Debbie was ignored by Denise, who thanked Mike.

The spa manager was speechless when we spent half the day rearranging treatments for the girls. My phone did not stop going with calls from the spa about the appointments. I just wanted to pack up and go home. Trying to do favours had been a disaster and from then on any celebrities that came out were given the spa number and asked to book for themselves. The Fortina also cut down the complimentaries to one treatment a day after Denise's trip.

The next problem was that we needed pictures in the spa, but would have to take them without disturbing the paying guests. The girls all happily agreed to get up early and shoot at eight o'clock, an hour before the spa opened. It was hard working in the heat of the spa and we were still there when it opened. With it being Denise's birthday, the girls were getting excitable and a little too noisy. As the spa guests were arriving, the spa manager, quite reasonably, asked me to get them to be quiet. But when I did ask them to keep it down a bit, Denise snapped: 'Shut up, Herr Flick!' This was her nickname for my army style of organising. It was the last straw and I went back to my room.

Later that morning she sent me a text, thanking me for sorting everything out. 'Love you, darling.' That's the only time Denise and I have fallen out; it must have been a mixture of her not drinking and the stress of her party and the fact that I was tired and stressed too. But it simply wasn't worth falling out over.

To add even more colour to the mix, the actress Wendy Richards of *EastEnders* happened to be staying at the hotel. The Fortina was her favourite getaway. Wendy's reputation as a formidable woman preceded her and I had heard from cast members she could be difficult. Rumours were rife about her leaving *EastEnders* and her cancer coming back and the paparazzi had started to stake out the hotel. Denise was not a fan of Wendy and the feeling was mutual. If they were in the same room they never acknowledged one another, nor did Wendy speak to the other actresses, preferring to spend time with her partner, John Burns, or the management of the hotel.

I'll never forget my first meeting with her. Smoking a cigarette by the pool, I was about to rejoin the girls when a red-faced Wendy came charging towards me in a white top. 'Oi, you! Any of your lot trying to take pictures of me on my balcony, tell them to back off,' she shouted, pointing her finger at me.

It seemed that the paps had gained access to the main body of the hotel and were trying to snap Ms Richards as she sunbathed by her private roof-top pool. Apparently I was guilty by association!

Having had enough of starlet tantrums, I snapped back, 'First of all my name is Steven, not Oi! I never work with paparazzi nor would anyone working with me disturb your time at the hotel in any way. Please get your facts right.' Ms Richards looked puzzled for a second, then, seeming not to know what to say, she muttered, 'Oh, OK then, have a nice evening,' and walked off.

Next day she looked less than pleased that John was chatting to me over breakfast. 'This is Steven,' he said. 'Yeah I know,' she replied, looking less than impressed. But everything changed when I asked about her dog and told her my dog Costa had died of cancer a few years back and suddenly this wonderful soft woman appeared, who I now wish I'd had more time with. I must say I shed a tear when I discovered she had died in 2009.

The birthday party that evening kicked off with Dee C Lee singing 'See the Day' to Denise and her guests, a cappella style. We had a great birthday dinner and the spread looked good in OK. Much as all the girls had been a delight, taking so many away is not for the faint-hearted. Having said that, Denise is still my favourite girl to work with.

12

Denise Denise

I had not seen much of Denise while I was in the States, but we kept in contact and had been out for dinner on my occasional visits to London. Her sister, Debbie, had stayed with me for two months when I lived in San Diego and Lester had come over for a few weeks during this time. He managed to fall over while cruising in Balboa Park and broke his arm, and also caught crabs (body lice). He and Debbie were on a trip to Beverly Hills, where they were sharing a room, and he'd had the cheek to send her into the chemist to buy some Quellada lotion, because he was too embarrassed to get it himself.

On their drive back to San Diego they managed to crash their hire car. Debbie was driving and the other car just ran into her. As Lester hobbled out of the passenger side, already bandaged on one arm and the other hand scratched with his infestation, the horrified driver gave in and admitted guilt immediately. He ended up comforting the shocked Lester who, true to form, made a complete drama of the whole thing.

Debbie was close to hysterics when they got back. I was hosting a dinner party for my two gay neighbours, Rick and Court. Rick had played Ernie in the touring version of *Sesame Street* and his boyfriend Court was an obnoxious ex-city banker. Being new to the area, though, I wanted the dinner to go well.

I suggested that Lester, who was quite shaken up, lie down and forget about the dinner but he insisted not only on coming but also 'helping' with everything. There was little for him to do and what he did help with he turned into a performance. I left a cupboard door open and, as he bent over to pick something out, he bashed his head on it. Blood running down his forehead, he glared at me as though I'd done it deliberately.

Debbie managed to cover the wound with a plaster and so, fortunately, he did not need another visit to A&E. Lester was now resembling Pudsey Bear, what with his broken arm, and we all felt sorry for him. The dinner went well and afterwards we decided to nip down to the local night-club. Lester, despite possibly having concussion, decided to come too and, as he got drunker, wandered around the night-club, saying, 'Hello, want to fuck a cripple?' Later he was found in the middle of the dance floor, bopping to 'The Pleasure Principle' by Janet Jackson. His antics had our American friends in fits of laughter, and we were an instant hit.

Denise and I talked on the phone a lot during that period, mainly to keep up with Lester's adventures and also to hear how Debbie was. Debbie had returned to working on cruise liners as a beautician; she often worked on the same ship as my sister, Karen, who was an on-board croupier.

Though I was thousands of miles away, I had managed to upset Denise's new husband, Tim Healy. He had recorded the message on their answerphone, but had such a heavy accent that I thought it was a joke message. So I left some rude comments along the lines that only a Geordie could have such a daft message on her phone. She was not best pleased and Tim thought I was taking the piss.

When she gave birth to their son, Matthew, I rang the hospital to congratulate her. 'Was it painful?' I asked. 'Steven, if a nurse had come in with a mallet and asked if I wanted to be hit on the head with it instead, I'd have begged her to,' Denise said, laughing. She always keeps her sense of humour in everything she does.

160

Lester kept me updated on Denise's post-natal depression and when she had bad turns I would call her or drop her a card. I wished I could be there in person and give her a big hug. Although the calls and cards allowed me to feel I was at least doing something, there's little anyone can do to help when someone is in the grips of depression. It always irritates me when people suffering from depression are told to count their blessings, or to consider all the starving people in Africa. The truth is that someone truly suffering from depression might win millions on the lottery but still feel bad.

Towards the end of my American adventure, I became really homesick for my mates and as soon as I was back in London, Denise and I were as thick as thieves again. I loved Tim and all was forgotten about my sarcastic phone message. Denise's career had gone from strength to strength and she had become a huge hit playing Marsha Stubbs in ITV's *Soldier Soldier*. She was starting to get stopped for autographs in the street when she was up north, though in London, where it's not uncommon to see stars, she could walk around without attracting attention.

On one of my first nights out back in London, Denise, Rose, Lester and I all went out for a bar crawl and ended up in The Yard, a popular gay bar in Soho. The place was really busy and we were teasing Denise after she told us she was getting stopped for autographs. Unknown to Denise, Lester and I dashed out to a corner shop and bought pens and pads; we waited until the music quietened down and then ran up to her like demented schoolgirls, screaming: 'Oh my God, it's Denise Welch from *Soldier Soldier*! Can we have your autograph please?'

Denise has always been a hit with gay guys so the bar erupted. Denise could have killed us, though the funny thing is that later in the evening two real fans stopped her halfway down Compton Street. When we parted for the night, Denise said, 'See, you two bitches!'

These days, when Denise walks down Compton Street, it's as if Madonna has arrived. 'We love you, Den, you're one of us,' scream the guys from GAY bar. Denise laps it up – she loves gay guys and their bars and the campness of it all.

Denise was back in my chair at Sweeny's, getting her high-lights done, when she told me she had been singing 'Walk on By' on *Soldier Soldier*. I asked why she did not have a record deal like Robson Green and Jerome Flynn, the two other stars of the show, and she let out a nervous little giggle, whispering that it might be in the pipeline.

Simon Cowell, who wasn't the megastar he is today, signed Denise up and her first single was to be a double A side – 'You Don't Have to Say You Love Me' and 'Cry Me a River'. The next time she came to have her roots done, she brought a demo tape. Now Denise has a good voice but to me the numbers felt out of date and I told her they needed modernising. I was a bit surprised when the single came out exactly the same as the demo. It beat Cher in the charts, entering at number 23, but then went straight out the next week. It was a real shame as she had a better voice than many of the singers in the charts and I think if she had been given a more modern number, perhaps some-thing in the Kylie style, she'd have done much better. I wished I had bleached her hair fully blonde and cut it short, a bit like Madonna on the cover of 'True Blue'.

I got my way many years later, although not without a fight, when Denise was starring in *Coronation Street*. She agreed to do her first really sexy shoot and, for once, the over-zealous Corrie press office stayed away. I dyed her hair fully blonde and cut it into a flatter, more modern look. Denise loves lots of height in her hair and I had to run up when she was in position for the photos and flatten it, as she'd constantly push it up at the crown when I wasn't looking.

Andrea Fone, who now works for police forensics doing

make-up from crime scenes, did Denise's make-up and we dressed her in sexy rubber and corsets. Celebrity photographer Alan Strutt shot the pictures and the men's magazine *Front* snapped them up. Denise laughed about becoming a glamour girl in her forties but they are the sexiest pictures she's ever had done. They would have been a brilliant look for Denise's record cover.

Rose Hirst was Denise's PA during the promotional tour for the record release, which was nearing the end when I went with my sister Karen and the Contessa (Pam Sharrock) to Soho House to celebrate with them. When we turned up, Denise looked awful: her stylish crochet trousers kept falling down and she was taking the girls to the toilets for 'talks' and slurring her words. To be honest, she was a bit of an embarrassment and it was the first time I had ever seen her like this. I put it down to the pressure of the record, but I was worried that it might all be getting too much for her.

Denise was sitting in my flat in Onslow Square the night before her audition with Brian Park and Judi Hayfield for *Coronation Street*. It was a huge role and we all got so excited. We were sure she was going to get it, but Denise refused to take anything for granted. She had days with Rose Hirst learning to pick up her Manchester accent and, as always, she was brilliant.

Sure enough, she got the part as *femme fatale* Natalie, and in 1997 she walked down the cobbled streets of Weatherfield and into *Coronation Street*. Natalie started a torrid affair with the much younger Kevin Webster, whose loving but dull wife, Sally, was away in Scarborough nursing her sick friend. All us gay lads thought she was a very lucky girl getting to snog Kevin, played by Michael Le Vell, though Denise could not share our enthusiasm, describing it as more like kissing a dead cat, something she repeated on *Loose Women* last year.

I travelled up to Manchester to do her hair for one of her first interviews with Jane Moore. Denise is great at making sure she looks after her friends work-wise. Jane Moore was also a great pal, so it was odd that Denise had to be flanked by one of the PR officers from the *Coronation Street* press office. We all had Denise's number and were free to talk to her at any time, but it felt strange to realise that things were going to be different now she was in *The Street*. Denise found it uncomfortable too, but did not want to rock the boat as she was new to the show. The press office usually sits in on interviews to protect the cast; sometimes it's necessary but on other occasions it is just the press office being jobsworths.

One time, Bev Callard, who plays Liz McDonald, was doing an interview with me and the PR person kept interrupting, and taking calls loudly on his mobile. At one point he stopped the conversation and handed the phone to Bev to do another interview over the phone. 'Only a quickie!' he shouted in the middle of the VA hotel bar. Bev leaned over and whispered to me, 'Let's meet up at five for a drink.' We met up and did the interview then, without the rude PR man. The press office is brilliant at *Coronation Street*, but sometimes they overdo it.

The beauty of *Coronation Street* is that some of the UK's best actors appear in it. They are extremely skilled at creating the illusion that they are not acting at all, something that's really hard to do. People who think that all you have to do is 'be yourself' should try picking up a script sometime and see if they can sound natural. When we turn on the box and tune into *Corrie*, we really feel as if we are looking into the lives of others. That's why it was such groundbreaking television when Tony Warren created it 50 years ago and why it's still going strong today.

That said, and much as Denise is an amazing actress, in some strange way her being in the show rather ruined it for me, as she was my best mate, not Natalie. I have to admit I was glad when she left, and Natalie is still my least favourite part Denise has played.

The great thing for me and Lester at the time was that Denise invited us to lots of the cast parties. One of the first we went to was Vicky Entwistle's birthday party, held at the VA hotel frequented by the cast. The party was great and there were loads of cast members there. It did seem weird seeing people that I had grown up watching on the box, and realising how different they were from their screen characters, even though I was used to working with actors and celebrities.

As the party continued, Lester handed me some coke and told me to take Denise for a line. We went up to my room – the 'Sooty and Sweep' room (all the rooms at the VA have a television theme). There was some champagne in the bucket still and we grabbed a glass each. I handed Denise the coke, but she shook her head and took me to the bathroom, where she laid out two large lines. 'Don't tell Lester I've had any or he'll tell everyone,' she said. She beckoned me over to take my line. It was only the third time I'd tried coke but, as I don't have an addictive personality, I felt fine about it and could take it or leave it. So I took it and we went back downstairs. At that point, I had no worries about Denise taking the occasional line of coke. She was a wonderful mother, and a great person who was always the first to do things for charity. I knew I could turn to her night or day if I had a problem. She had been fighting depression and if a bit of coke cheered her up then what the hell?

We had many a night out with Vicky and Denise in London. One particular evening, Denise, Jane Moore, Vicky and I were all in a minicab after partying at Soho House, when the driver knocked over a man just outside the Sports Bar in Haymarket. To our horror, our cabbie tried to drive off just as the man was managing to pick himself up. But the lights were red and our cab was surrounded by an angry group of people who had witnessed the incident. The girls were all terrified but, after checking the pedestrian was OK, I managed to get them all out and into another cab.

Minutes later, driving along the Embankment, a police car stopped the second driver. We were all sure we were going to be arrested for leaving the scene of a crime. Instead they wanted to check the driver's details. The girls, being well plastered, started to flirt with the very good-looking police officers, who clearly found it amusing though they asked them to be quiet. Meanwhile, headlines kept flashing through my mind: 'Corrie girls in hit and run horror.' With two such well-known actresses in the car it was really funny when one officer said: 'Hey, are you Jane Moore from *The Sun*?' Jane was thrilled and flirted away, telling them we were off to a party and giving them the address. I was just waiting for her to be put in cuffs.

Thankfully the police sent us all on our way and we got to Lester's place in Battersea for the party. An hour later there was a knock on the door; imagine my horror when I looked down and saw the police officers, this time in civilian dress. They had taken Jane up on her offer to come to the party! Lester thought all his dreams had come true as the handsome men walked in. Vicky's mouth dropped open. 'I don't believe it,' she said. Vicky is lovely but can turn into a different person when she drinks, not one that is pleasant to be around.

The first time I ever really rock 'n' roll partied was at the Mr Gay UK contest. I had spent my twenties being a good husband to Martin, who hated clubbing, and now, in my thirties, I was enjoying going out, while Martin played bridge and enjoyed dinner parties. Denise and my friend Anna Ryder Richardson were judging the show in Leeds, so I went up to join them. The other guests were Sir Ian McKellen and Cynthia Payne, the madam made famous by the film *Personal Services*.

There were drinks before the show and Cynthia and Anna were there with local gay VIPs. We started to drink heavily, mainly due to nerves, as the cameras were snapping not only Denise but anyone associated with her. Cynthia Payne turned out to be a right bore; nothing like the Julie Walters character in the film. She kept going on about getting food and Lester quipped: 'Maybe she's run out of luncheon vouchers.'

We were legless by the time the judging started and we partied afterwards late into the night at the Hilton hotel. I managed to grab two hours sleep before we all met in reception to go home. We were all still wasted. Anna had managed to pick up the only straight security guard at the show – he was gorgeous and we were all jealous. Denise asked us all to come back to Wilmslow, where she was living at the time. I ummed and ahhed about it but Denise told me stop being so sensible and start enjoying myself. Her husband Tim had often asked me to stay too so I said yes.

Everyone jumped in their cars and headed to the King's Arms pub – and I mean everyone – Anna, her security guard, a friend of his, the designer Stewart Parvin, who makes clothes for the Queen, and some of the contestants from the Mr Gay UK contest.

Tim was in the pub when we got there, and I don't think the locals had ever seen anything like it. One of the men in the pub said loudly: 'All these lads are gay.' Matthew, Denise's son, was staying with his grandparents, so we partied the day away, mainly in the car park. Denise then decided to take it back to her place, though Tim was in a foul mood when we all got there and took himself off to bed. Denise went up to see what was wrong and suddenly I heard her shout, 'Steve, Steven, Steven!'

I thought perhaps Tim was hitting her and I charged upstairs to the bedroom. There she was, standing over the bed with a lampshade in her hand, about to hit Tim. He asked all of us to leave so I took Denise downstairs, wondering why she'd called for me rather than the burly security guard. Tim had been drinking whisky, which brings out the worst in him but, in his defence, having half of Mr Gay UK arriving in the middle of your quiet Sunday would be too much for most people.

I was cross about being asked to leave, as Tim had been on and on about me staying the weekend there. But I drove home with Stewart and a couple of others and, as I sobered up, I realised that two-day benders might suit Status Quo, but they are not for me. And they are not really for Denise either as in the long run it only makes her depression worse.

I was with her at the BBC one day, walking along a corridor, when an excited voice shouted: 'It is you, it is you, I love you!' We looked round and were amazed to see Sir Cliff Richard, who ran up to Denise and hugged her. He had a quick chat, and wanted to talk more but he had an engagement. He is a huge fan of *Coronation Street*. Denise just stood there, open-mouthed, as he walked off. 'Thank God you were here, Steven. Nobody would believe me if I told them Cliff is such a fan of mine,' she laughed. Denise just did not see how big she was becoming.

Another fan of Denise's was the young BBC presenter, Richard Bacon. He sat on the floor of the BBC green room VIP section looking up at her like a little puppy, talking ten to the dozen. Denise was really nervous, because she was releasing the balls for the *National Lottery Live* show. She was practically shaking, but was polite to Richard. But we all wondered what he was on to be so hyper. Despite Denise being a wreck, she walked on and stole the show with her line: 'I play Natalie Barnes, who has always been great with balls, so I have no worries releasing them.' Everyone erupted.

Denise is an amazing mum, and has brought up an incredible son in Matthew, a bright boy who called Lester 'Aunty Lester' and was great fun to be with. He's talented too, though he and Denise had the usual mother and son stand-offs about home-work. With his musical talents, he was never going to be a doctor, but Denise was keen on him getting a good education. She is very proud of him.

When I heard she was pregnant again, I must admit I did not jump for joy. It was a little late in life and she had suffered terribly with depression after Matthew was born. It happened on a romantic weekend in Amsterdam with Tim, and I of course told her I was thrilled to bits for her, though I was worried.

Louis was born with Hirschsprung's disease, which is when a section of the bowel is essentially paralysed. He had to have seven inches of his intestine chopped out but, thank God, the operation was a success, and Denise and Tim have another wonderful, unique son. Louis can do all sorts of accents and dance moves, and if there is such a thing as reincarnation, then he must have been a comedian in a previous life.

Denise and I took him to Hurghada in Egypt for a photo assignment for *Hello Magazine* and he was hysterically funny throughout the trip even though he was only five at the time. At one point Denise and I were trying to work out whether the rep for the company was gay or straight and Louis must have overheard. Later that evening at dinner, Louis asked him whether he had a girlfriend. The rep said no, to which the five-year-old Louis replied: 'So you're gay then. Steven and Mum were wondering.'

Denise's biggest mistake was when she was appearing on *Down to Earth*, a show set on a country farm. I went to do a job with her on the set, and Lester told me she was having a thing with one of the crew. Denise knew that it was becoming common knowledge; most things were, once Lester knew. The minute Denise discreetly pointed out who it was, I could see that Steve Murray was trouble.

She was going through a bad time with Tim and wanted to tell me all about it in her trailer. I took the opportunity to have a quick pee, and settled down to have a chat. After five minutes

Denise complained of damp feet, then I realised mine were soaked too. I had flushed the toilet the wrong way and flooded her whole trailer. Typically, she thought it was hilarious and told all the crew and actors. I was relieved it was only a quick wee...

So the least of my worries was getting the facts about this Steve fella, who was a carpenter on the set and not exactly Brad Pitt. I had no idea what she was playing at. I liked Tim and hated the idea that I would be seeing him, knowing what she was doing with this carpenter. I did not approve and stayed away when I heard he was going to be around. I truly believe that Tim and Denise are soul mates, but perhaps they just like other toys to play with now and again.

I did not come face to face with Steve until the night of Denise's award-winning role as Mari Hoff in *Little Voice* at the Royal Exchange in Manchester. On the way up she rang to ask me for a favour; would I come for dinner with Steve and his family so she could get out of staying with him. Pleased that it sounded like it was over, I agreed.

Denise was amazing in *Little Voice* and it was the role of a lifetime. It was the same night that Jordan was voted out of the jungle on *I'm a Celebrity ... Get Me Out of Here*, so it was a double celebration. Steve was friendly and his family were nice. Once we got to dinner, Steve became so clingy towards Denise I began to feel rather sick. I couldn't understand how she could stand it. He kept asking her to come to his hotel but she said she couldn't as she had me staying but he kept asking her.

Even as we were saying goodbye in the street, Steve was trying to get her to come with him. She drove me to the VA and when we got there I broke my rule about not interfering in other people's business, and read her the Riot Act about him. She agreed it was time to call it off.

But it was a slow break-up and even though Denise only stayed at my fortieth birthday party for an hour, as she had another engagement, Steve came too and stayed on. My party was at the exclusive Monte's club in Sloane Street and was in aid of When You Wish Upon a Star, a charity that takes terminally ill kids to Lapland to see Santa. It's run by my dear friends Joanne and Pat Wright. Nicola Wheeler got me involved with it a few years back, and Denise has accompanied the kids on the trip for the past four years. Instead of birthday presents, I asked people to donate to the charity.

The club was packed with friends and celebrities, and Tamer Hassan, the hard-man movie actor, kicked off with a sizeable cheque. Nicola Wheeler got everyone to put in and we raised over £4,000. I bumped into Steve in the loo and he started to ask about Denise. I was a little drunk and told him that their affair was a bad idea. He went mad: 'Do not put that thought in her head,' he spat viciously. There was real anger in his eyes and it was pretty frightening.

It was a real relief when they split. I was working on my roof garden when I had a call from a number I didn't recognise. 'Hey, it's Steve,' a voice said. 'Steve who?' I asked. He told me and I immediately thought he must be calling to have a go at me. But no, he wanted to take some friends to Monte's club and wanted me to get them signed in. He asked me down too. I've no idea how he got my number and he muttered something about me giving it to him. I told him I would ring him back but never did.

As I feared from the start, he was trouble. A year later he spilled the beans on Denise in the *Mail on Sunday* and it was awful. I told Denise that all she could do was laugh and forget about it. It was a silly interview and at least he said she was good in bed! 'Tomorrow's fish and chip paper, Den,' I told her. Thank God he was gone.

It was nice when my next job was for the *News of the World*'s Sunday Magazine, taking Denise, Tim, Matthew, Louis, and Denise's sister, Debbie, her police officer husband Peter and their three children to the Tunisian town of Hammamet. Believe it or not, *Coronation Street* is very popular over there, and Julie Goodyear had stayed at the hotel a month before. Some of the locals would come up to Denise and say, 'Julie Goodyear'. Denise thought she was being mistaken for Julie, which made me laugh, as she is a lot prettier and younger than Julie. I think it was a relief when she realised they were just telling her Julie had stayed there.

It was my first job with the celebrity photographer Jamie Hughes, who had worked with the likes of Vin Diesel, Ben Affleck and Martin Scorsese. And now he was going to shoot Mr and Mrs Healy! It was the beginning of an interesting friendship, as we worked together for the next few years on many trips and shoots.

With everyone tired and even party girl Denise in bed, Jamie and I were left wanting a drink. Jamie is married to Sandra and has three children, but he is as vain as any gay man. He has his eyelashes tinted, sun-kissed highlights and wears all the latest Abercrombie & Fitch gear, so he looked rather like a straight version of me.

We went over the road to a small bar, where we were greeted like old pals by the owner, and given a free bottle of wine. 'You are with *Coronation Street*, you are my guest.' A group of young men waved over to us, and we felt like stars.

No sooner had we finished the wine than the boys sent another bottle over and asked to join us. They complimented us on how fit we looked, and one felt the muscles in Jamie's leg. 'I do a bit of kick boxing and work out,' Jamie said. I realised the lads wanted a bit more than just a drink but Jamie had no idea. His face fell when, a bit later, it finally dawned on him. When we left the bar, they followed us in their car and asked to come for a drive. 'No thanks,' Jamie squeaked. We laughed about it and Jamie and I became good friends after that.

Denise never looked happier than on that trip. She was great on the shoot, and Tim had me in tears of laughter. Denise is at her best when she has her loved ones around her, and when we celebrated Matthew's fourteenth birthday party at the hotel, there could not have been a happier or prouder mother than Denise Welch.

13

Coke and Cointreau

Lester Middlehurst was a brilliant journalist; his unique talent lay in getting celebrities to talk where others failed, which he usually did by talking about his own life and making them feel like a long-lost friend – or by plying them with champagne.

Writing had started to really interest me; I too seemed to have a natural flair for getting people to speak and the ability to tell a story. Hairdressing was not as challenging to me any more and I realised that it was all a bit of an illusion; if you have a bob, you can often get the same cut from a stylist who's just gradu-ated from a Sassoon apprenticeship as you would from a £200-plus celebrity stylist. There are many equally good stylists working in small towns and only charging £30. I'm not knocking celebrity stylists, but many women feel they are getting the best by paying outrageous prices, when often the only difference might be a head massage and a cappuccino, and sometimes not even that. Perhaps if you are having your hair cut from long to short it can be a good investment – or perhaps you simply have money to burn.

Make-up never really interested me, and my hands tended to shake when I applied false eyelashes or lip liner. I often did men's grooming and I could certainly powder down a shiny face. One of the funniest jobs I ever did was grooming for four men's magazine editors, who were mimicking the poses that women perform for them. Piers Hernu, who edited *Front* magazine, wore a green G-string, but had a bit of a spotty botty so I needed to cover stick it. Piers had a great sense of humour, but getting to the bottom of make-up, men's or women's, was not for me. I wanted to do something else.

Both Lester and Jane Moore suggested I do celebrity interviews. My column was good and, unlike many hairdressers and plastic surgeons, I wrote it myself and also came up with great feature ideas. Working often for 12 hours a day doing hair was taking its toll and I didn't want to be standing all day doing clients for the rest of my life.

Having watched Lester and Jane in action, I decided to give it a go and took to writing like a duck to water. I could still look after my good clients and come up with ideas for celebrities and often do their hair on the shoot too. Many hairdressers branch out into other arenas: Anthony Mascolo from Toni and Guy is a brilliant photographer and Martyn Fletcher moved into writing and make-up after managing Alan International. So becoming a journalist was not out of reach, and with a lot of help from Helen Galley, who trained journalists and had been a good friend since my Brighton days, it was time for a change.

Jane Moore was a busy columnist and had stepped down as editor of *The Sun*'s 'Woman' section. Sam Howard had married Ian Phillips, the commercial and marketing director for Jordan Grand Prix. She had left *The Sun* though she did some freelance styling work. Tiring of the fickle world of fashion, she later packed it in and now lives in a beautiful farmhouse in Oxford and is teaching at a boys' school. I often joke that she has not moved far – she was dealing with naughty boys at *The Sun* too. Sue Carroll, meanwhile, had moved to *The Mirror* where she would have her own column.

Most of my allies were gone, and I felt the new fashion editor was not a patch on Sam and it would not be long before they gave me the push as hairdressing columnist. I jumped instead and set up my own company putting features together, as well as representing one or two make-up artists. It was a gamble, but my first feature was 'A Question of Sex', in which I asked three stars personal questions about their sex lives. The stars were Denise Welch, Lauren Booth and Sam Robson from ITV's *The Bill*. It was a little saucy and I sent it to Amanda Cable, an old mate from *The Sun* who was now editor of the *Sunday People* magazine. She freely admits when she heard about my feature that she loved the idea but dreaded seeing the copy, as she only knew me as *The Sun* hairdresser. When she saw the words she was straight on the phone to buy it from me – and what's more, she wanted more interviews and feature ideas ASAP! Having good contacts in any job is half the battle and I was a regular party boy, always out meeting people while she was a mum who spent her nights at home. So I could network and talk people into interviews, not just for Amanda, but also for many others.

Stars can be demanding and, though Denise Welch is far from being a real diva, she insists whenever I see her that I give her a massage or foot rub. Even on our visit to Lapland with Wish Upon a Star last Christmas, halfway through the flight she sat on my knee and whined: 'Back rub please!' Denise had worked three days non-stop and dashed up from London to Humberside airport with her beautiful *Dancing on Ice* partner, American-born Matt Evers. We'd had three hours sleep and, with just the back massage to keep her going, she had chatted with parents and children till she landed back home that night. She then snatched four hours sleep and was up and off to train for *Dancing on Ice*. So I was happy to give her the massage, particularly as it does not lead to what she calls 'jiggy jiggy'. According to her, all straight men want sex two minutes into a massage. The nearest I have got to sex with her was French kissing at a gay club to wind Lester up, pretending that I was having 'a straight moment'.

It worked and he got cross about Denise wanting to sleep with me, and not him, and charged off.

However, whilst working with her in Marbella on one of my first hair/writing jobs, I did object to being blackmailed into giving her a foot massage at 8.30 in the morning, otherwise she wouldn't get up. This was despite promising me the previous evening that, if we went for a quiet dinner in Puerto Banus, she would be up and ready at eight. She'd promised a quiet dinner but I'd suffered a near death experience; you'd think she'd have been more flexible.

Denise and I had flown into Corrie del Sol along with her on-screen sister, Gabrielle Glaister. My idea was a piece on how many of the cast of *Corrie* either lived or had second homes in the Costa del Sol. Denise's good mate, Beverly Callard, also agreed to take part in the shoot the next day. We were having a quiet night in, with a few cocktails, when Denise decided it would be much nicer to nip down to Puerto Banus and have dinner at Aretusa, one of the area's finest restaurants. We'd be back in bed by midnight, she said.

It was all going to plan when one of the nicest people in show business, Barbara Windsor, with her husband, Scott Mitchell, who I get on with like a house on fire, walked into the restaurant along with some of the *EastEnders* cast, including the glamorous Rula Lenska, who was featuring in the show. Next Beverly Callard swanned in, full of energy and ready to party. My heart fell – neither Denise nor I can say no to a great night out. 'We must be in bed by midnight,' we murmured, half-heartedly. Luckily, though, the cast of *EastEnders* had to be up early to film so after a brilliant dinner they took off. By this time Denise had her 'Please let's party more!' face on, and the bright lights were calling. Beverly suggested we go for a quick one at Bob's Bar in the Puerto.

The next thing I knew it was midnight and instead of being safely tucked up in bed I was boarding a boat with Beverly

Callard, a friend of hers who was the captain's son, his girlfriend, Denise and Gabrielle – and a few bottles of champagne.

It was not long before we were at sea. The clothes came off and most of us were in the water, which was blissfully warm for November. Climbing back on board, it didn't seem to matter that there was a photographer expected at eight in the morning with a make-up girl in tow; after all, how many times can you say you're with the cast of *Corrie*, sipping champagne, swimming and having a blast on a private boat?

The water was so beautiful Gabrielle and I stripped back off and were joined by the captain for a last swim. We went a little way from the boat and I was just glancing back when to my horror I heard the engine start and the boat took off, leaving us naked in the middle of the ocean.

Gabrielle is a petite, pretty blonde and I look like the Jolly Green Giant next to her. She tried to console me: 'Don't worry, Steve. I'm an Olympic-standard swimmer; I'll get us back to shore.' I was not filled with confidence and the thought of sharks made me worry even more.

Plus there was the inconvenient fact that I was buck naked, so if we were rescued by a passing ship, or made it to land, it was going to be a very embarrassing entrance. It was like some hideous nightmare and suddenly the sea felt a lot colder. Five minutes in the water seemed like an hour – and then I stopped swimming and almost went under, but that was because I was so excited at seeing the boat return. It had all been a little joke by the captain's son.

Denise was crying when I got back on board: 'I nearly pooped myself when I came up on deck and saw you had been left,' she said.

'Oh dear, I am sorry you were upset, what the fuck do you think I was feeling?' was my response. Needless to say it was time to head to shore.

It was 4.30 in the morning when we got home to Denise's apartment, and we made it to bed by five. I was up at eight to greet the photographer, Jason Buckner, and the make-up woman, but getting Denise up was a nightmare. In the end I gave in to the blackmail and rubbed her feet. Just as she was relaxing into the massage, I grabbed her ankles and pulled her out of bed, which served her right.

The bright young things from Brighton were by now a lot older and in some cases not much wiser. Denise's career was going from strength to strength, but her dark depressions and often out-of-control partying were becoming a worry. We were all party animals really. Lester loved to be centre of attention and had a real need for approval and love, which I believe stemmed from having been adopted and also having spent years at boarding school. It left him very needy, and, being a sexual predator, he would stay somewhere, even when they started mopping the floors, until he found a man for the night, preferably a straight one.

I remember Denise talking about being taken to parties by her parents, and just wanting to go home. She told me about her sixteenth birthday party, when her mum wore an amazing cat suit, and the boys all arrived, handed Denise her gifts, and then hung out with her mum instead. Maybe she thought parties were an important part of life and that she had something to prove. Even recently, when we had been at dinner with Ingrid Tarrant at La Poule au Pot, while Ingrid headed off home, Tom Hopkins, the theatre producer, suggested going on and right away Denise agreed. 'You're a long time dead,' she said. 'You can't go to Sainsbury's or have drinks with mates when you're gone!' I merely enquired as to the last time she had been in Sainsbury's. The upshot was she left me at 3am and yet was on *Loose Women* that lunchtime full of energy, while I felt like death.

People think that being a hairdresser is a light, fluffy job. Really! I would love them to find out what back-breaking and exhausting work it can be for a busy stylist. If I am working the next day I do not party heavily – it's not fair on the paying customer. You are touching people more than in most other service industries and good hairdressers in America have their nails manicured to perfection and watch what they eat, as they are breathing over people. Once you become a celebrity stylist you are invited to loads of parties and I found the best way to deal with this was to turn up, show my face and, after a suitable length of time, go to the toilet and head for the exit with the minimum of fuss, avoiding the peer pressure to make me stay later than I want.

By the late nineties, something dark and sinister had entered our group – coke. I was always very anti-drugs and I loathed pot. Whenever it was around it seemed to ruin things. On one occasion, the gang, which by this time included the Contessa, who had become a firm friend, all went to Amsterdam to celebrate Lester's birthday, though Denise was not with us on that occasion. We kicked off the proceedings early afternoon with a trip to one of the famous Dutch coffee shops. The lads all smoked some super-skunk, while the ladies opted for skunk cake. One of the local Dutch lads suggested that they only have a small piece but the girls, including some female journalists, were a bossy lot and dismissed his advice.

Two hours later most of us were giggling wrecks. Later that evening, though Martin and I were down ready to go to Lester's birthday dinner, there was no sign of the rest of them. Eventually an exhausted Mr Middlehurst appeared, then the bleary-eyed Contessa, followed by her then husband, Ian Sharrock, and a still giggling Rosemary Hirst. The rest had passed out in bed. By the time the Indonesian banquet had finished, Martin, me and Lester's former partner, Paul Cooper, were all that was left from the original party. The rest had given up the ghost because of the skunk.

By the next morning, when we returned to London, some of our party had spent almost the entire weekend in bed – what a waste of money and time, and all due to taking drugs.

Lester rang me early one Wednesday morning. He was due to have his blue-black hair tint done on Thursday evening and was very excited about something. 'Darling, have you ever done this coke thing? Everyone is doing it!' he said. Lester went on to say he had been out with some of the *Coronation Street* crowd who had been at it; he had been tempted but wanted to have a try with me as he felt safer. Automatically I said no, that it was a very bad idea and that he would be the one to get hooked. Lester, thinking quickly, pointed out that we had tried dope together and he was not hooked on that. And anyway he was going to do it with or without me.

It made no difference when I told him I had tried it once by accident with Gavin and it did nothing for me but made me chew and talk a lot. I knew when Lester was on a mission; there would be no stopping him. So I agreed we would both try it after doing his hair on the Thursday, before going to the *Daily Mail* party. It was one of the worst ideas of our lives.

It was not difficult to find coke in London. Everyone had a dealer or a friend who knew a dealer. So on the Thursday Lester, with all the enthusiasm of a child opening a Christmas present, could not wait to get tucked in. I applied the tint to his hair and explained only to take small lines from the coke and to go easy with it. Nipping out to the pub to get a couple of drinks, I was gone around 20 minutes. On my return Lester was talking at a hundred miles an hour down the phone to the Contessa: 'I am doing this coke thing, and it's done nothing to me!' To my horror, he had snorted almost the whole of his gram while I had been out.

Lester would not listen to my warnings that he was as high as a kite, and wanted me to let him have some of mine, 'to really see if it works'. Moving on to the party, where there were loads of *Daily Mail* staff, I explained that he must try to control his talking. 'Yeah, yeah,' was his only response.

Later I could see the renowned *Daily Mail* critic Jack Tinker struggling to get away from Lester who just could not stop talking to him. Lester had always been desperate to be best friends with Jack but, though always polite, Jack was not a fan of Lester and found his behaviour in the office loud, disruptive and overtly gay. I tried to get Lester away, and had a quick chat with the relieved Jack, only to be talked over by Lester. Eventually Jack put his hand up. 'I am listening to Steven now,' he snapped. Lester, put out, moved off. Even the brilliant columnist Baz Bamigboye, one of Lester's greatest allies, came up and asked what Lester was on as he was driving them all mad.

Getting him to leave the party was not easy. Eventually I made up a story about it being a special night at Brompton's, a gay club in Earls Court, and he agreed to leave. He kept repeating that the coke had done nothing to him.

Even the next day Lester rang me rambling on about how disappointing the coke was and what a waste of money. That was a relief, as he was truly awful on it. I left it and decided not to do a party post-mortem. Later though he told me there had been comments in the office about his outrageous behaviour that night.

Coke didn't raise its head again for a while but six months later Lester rang when he was partying with Denise and some *Corrie* cast members at Soho House. He was doing coke: 'It's really good. The stuff we tried must not have worked. Come down and join us,' he said. It was a school night, so I politely declined. Denise rang me the next day and told me that he had again been a bit of a nightmare on coke.

Coke really appeals to the creative types – actors and musicians have hectic schedules, and being under the scrutiny of the public eye can become too much and they turn to coke for confidence and to keep them awake. One young actress once told me that singing or performing for her mother and father when she was a child had made her feel special and that it had been the time when they had paid her the most attention. 'It is what drove me to entertain,' she said, 'but when hundreds of people thought they knew me, and how I was feeling, it was terrifying. When a fellow cast member offered me a line of coke I wasn't sure, but after a few lines I felt like the star everyone thought I was, and could face the public with confidence. Eventually I never went to a first-night party or event without charlie in my handbag.'

But it is a false confidence; you will always pay a price for something that is not real. I've heard people say that it helps their depression; well, it might do that for one night but it will always make things ten times worse the next day. It can destroy creative talent, not to mention the damage to your health and looks with long-term use.

It was Tallulah Bankhead who once said: 'Cocaine isn't addictive. I should know, I've been taking it all my life.' It's an amusing quote but within it lies the danger of cocaine – people who take it are almost always in denial about what it is doing to them.

A few months later we were all having a fantastic night at Soho House; the hilariously funny Phil Middlemiss, who played Des Barnes in *Coronation Street*, was there, along with his date, the gorgeous Alison King, who now plays Carla Conor. She was stunning and at the time was appearing in *Dream Team*, a show about footballers. With looks like that, I wondered why she was not a huge star. But she had a right mood on that night. One of Alison's friends had had a very private area pierced, and she was taking the girls to the ladies to have a look. Denise was really keen to see it – she had recently had her belly button pierced in a bit of a rush during her lunch break. As she had laid down, she had asked, 'Does it hurt?' Then they'd started and she'd let out an almighty scream: 'OH FUCK!'

All the talk of female genitalia and the like had all the straight guys quite excited and, as always, there was talk of girl-on-girl action. Alison piped up: 'Shut up, how about boy-on-boy action?' The very straight Phil Middlemiss was only too happy to oblige and grabbed me, sticking his tongue down my throat. It was a little too realistic for the moody Alison, who stomped off in a huff. Sadly, Phil was one of the best kissers I have come across. Jane Moore's outrageous husband was one of the others. He once grabbed me to prove to Lester that you did not have to be gay to kiss a fella. It did not prove anything – but Lester was pissed off that it was me that he kissed.

It was not long before some of the partygoers wanted coke. Denise confessed that she had been doing it for a while, but thought she might be doing too much; she was going to stop after tonight. We both agreed that Lester on it was a bad idea. He was indiscreet and flamboyant after a few Cointreaus on the rocks; coke gave him the platform to move to a whole new level of bad behaviour, including coming on to straight men, whether they liked it or not.

He started to introduce me as his 'dizzy, dyslexic blond hair-dresser, who now writes for papers, and introduced me to drugs'. Of course this was completely untrue (he had done that all by himself), and the fact that I had also taken him to the gym and yoga classes never seemed to come into it. Nor that I'd helped him get some charity work with the AIDS kitchen, delivering food to people who were suffering, something he did until the week he died. Luckily, he only behaved like this when he was drunk, and people ignored him, but I could have happily strangled him.

Later that month Lester was offered a huge pay rise by Richard

Desmond to move to *The Express* as chief celebrity reporter. Much as the *Daily Mail* has a reputation for being homophobic, Lester had always been treated well and had become a bit of an icon there. The paper was like his family and editor Paul Dacre had become like a father to him. Dacre was someone Lester looked up to; he was a figure that provided stability, telling Lester off when he was bad and sending him congratulations when he did a great interview. In a way, this was more important to Lester than money.

Lester had once handed in his notice a few years back, but after a fatherly chat with Dacre he had instead been offered his own chat show on *Channel One* (owned by The Daily Mail group) called *One to One with Lester Middlehurst*. I don't think he ever really wanted to leave; he just wasn't getting enough attention that month.

Sadly, the show was a disaster as the outrageous Lester turned into a wooden puppet in front of the cameras, barely moving throughout the interviews. He did get some great guests though, and even Jackie Collins appeared on the show.

I threw a party for his first episode and asked Liam Hamilton from LWT along to watch in the hope he might use Lester. Liam's only comment was that the set moved several times and that maybe with a bit of training on a regional station Lester could do some presenting. Lester was livid, and called Liam all sorts of names behind his back, but Liam was right.

Lester preferred to concentrate on the one good review he got – in the *Daily Mail*, which, of course, owned the show. 'Lester Middlehurst is the new Russell Harty,' which was exactly the phrase Lester had used about himself. There were no other positive reviews. I never once told Lester the show was no good, nor what people said about it; much as he could be cruel and cutting about my work or what people said, he was too insecure and sensitive himself to handle the truth.

The show never ran another season, but Lester's thirst for TV never wavered; he even stooped so low as to go on GMTV and claim that he was a good friend of Freddie Mercury. Towards the end of Lester's life he told people he was writing a biography and the opening line was, 'The night I slept with Freddie Mercury.' I think he might have met him once, at a party with Kenny Everett, but, trust me, if Lester really had slept with him, I would have heard all about it.

Lester's obsession with fame and celebrity was becoming unhealthy. He was not willing to train in anything and, being surrounded by friends in the spotlight, he felt he had a right to be a famous TV personality. He thought a move to *The Express*, which would also mean writing for *OK Magazine*, would catapult him into a position that would get him on television. At *The Mail* he was one of many little fish but at *The Express* he was going to be a big fish. Desmond had certainly massaged Lester's ego.

Having worked on shoots with many different publications, I knew that Northern & Shell, which owned *The Express*, never seemed in a rush to pay freelancers and they were not my favourite group to work for. They seemed to hire quality journalists but many later left or were pushed. A week before Lester was due to join *The Express*, I rang to tell him of my concerns. That was a mistake, as I got shot down within minutes and Lester hung up on me. Later that night he rang, drunk, to tell me he loved me, he knew I was only being a friend, and that he had his doubts himself, but, what the fuck, you only live once!

Lester's demands that he be allowed to smoke in *The Express* offices, and his behaviour in general, did not go down well there. Add to that his constant need for attention, and his champagne expense account, and it was never going to work out. After just 18 months he parted company with them and, in the second biggest mistake of his life, he went freelance.

Being a freelance in any field takes a lot of self-discipline, particularly in journalism. You need to get yourself up early, and get your own interviews. Editors will not use you if they have a staff member that can do the job so you have to set things up yourself. Meanwhile, Lester's coke problem was getting worse. He would never turn up for a night out without at least a gram on him, and he was drinking heavily, going through two bottles of wine, or gallons of Kir Royale or Bellinis and a bottle of Cointreau a night.

His mother, Heather, passed away, leaving Lester a small fortune. He bought a beautiful home in Battersea, with two pubs a stone's throw away – the Castle and the Woodman. He took himself off on several holidays to prepare himself for his new self-employed career.

In Battersea he found a whole new group of friends who would party into the small hours. He didn't hang out as much at Soho House and became even more unreliable. It was not long before he was living a vampire-like existence. He would ring me at nine in the morning, slurring his words. When I asked if he had been to bed, like most addicts he would lie and say yes, of course he had. Then he would confess that he had been up all night and tell me the story of the straight lad just out of prison that he had spent all night seducing.

Really I wish none of us had ever tried coke, and we could turn the clock back to when having a few drinks was enough. Lester was turning into an embarrassment – he was funny enough just drinking coffee, yet he thought he needed drugs and alcohol to get by.

Once, I was with Denise in Spain when she received a call from a new female friend, whom she'd met in a bar in Knightsbridge. During the phone call, her new friend had asked if Denise could give her the number of her dealer in London but Denise did not have it on her.

She was excited about her new friend, who had been visiting London from Dubai, where she had a business with her husband. They were huge fans of *Coronation Street* and still watched it on digital TV. Denise and this new friend had got on famously when they'd met. For the woman it had been a rare night out on the town with her nanny.

Denise had been partying with Lester and his then boyfriend, whom they nicknamed Murder Mark, as everyone hated him, except me; I just felt indifferent towards him. With them was another of Lester's friends, Chris the Greek. It was a nice surprise when the woman sent over a magnum of champagne.

Denise and Lester cannot resist new people so of course they invited the woman and her nanny to join them. After a while the woman said how she liked to party and liked the odd line or E. Denise, being naive and always wanting to be everyone's best friend, piped up: 'Oh, I love a line but I don't like Es.' She talked openly about how she knew someone who could get it for her, and the woman asked whether she could get his number at some point. Denise and Lester then left to go to Soho House.

Back in Spain Denise called her new friend later that night as she wanted to invite her to a party later that week. The number went dead, which Denise thought was a little odd, but perhaps the phone was stolen.

A week later, on a Saturday, a very upset Denise rang me. The *Sunday Mirror* had called her to say they were running a Denise takes drugs story on the front page. The woman, Denise's new friend, had been an undercover journalist.

Denise was in the country for the weekend with her family and so wanted me to get the paper in the morning. I got up at 6am and went to Victoria Station to get it – and it couldn't have been much worse. My heart was sinking as I read it to her, though she stayed calm as she asked me to read several paragraphs again. Then she said, 'Thanks, darling,' and hung up.

By Friday a dark depression had set in and she rang me in tears. 'I am not a bad person, am I, Steven?' she asked. She certainly wasn't – Denise works tirelessly for charity, has raised two amazing kids and is loved by millions. Like any human being, she has her weaknesses. But I was worried about her mental health in the aftermath of the article.

When we got together at my place she talked openly about the coke and her drinking, and vowed that she was giving it all up. That night, when I joined her and Lester at Soho House, she was talking nineteen to the dozen so I took her to one side and asked her if she was on the charlie. She swore that she wasn't – but 20 minutes later I saw her pass it back to Lester.

Later, though, after suffering a breakdown while playing the wicked queen in pantomime, Denise went for help and gave up drugs and drink. It was a brave thing to do and once she had kicked them she never looked better or happier. I don't know if the drugs and alcohol added to her mental problems but they certainly can't have helped.

Lester, however, was having none of it. 'I love coke!' he declared. 'If I give up drink and drugs, I'll be boring. All my friends do it.'

I got the name of a good drug counsellor from Daniella Westbrook, who had battled her own addiction problems. She was careful to say that what suits one person might not suit another, however. He started going to counselling but, sure enough, after four sessions Lester gave up. All he seemed to get from it was that technically everyone he knew was an addict.

There were other attempts at therapy but they wanted to send him straight to rehab, which made Lester run a mile. He had met an addict in the pub who said he had been twice and it never works. There was worse news in that he had found a doctor who had prescribed him sleeping pills and antidepressants. Lester was already getting sleeping pills from a doctor friend of his, and much as the private doctor had told him he could have a glass of wine on the antidepressants, he was continuing to drink heavily on them and do up to two or three grams of charlie, staying up for several days at a time.

It was hard for his real friends to be with him when he was like that and he would cause trouble everywhere he went. He told awful stories about Denise to her nearest and dearest, to punish her for not dropping everything when he called. We started not including him at parties and evenings out for fear of the damage he would cause.

Lester told a friend he was being so mean to his real friends to push us away, so when he committed suicide we would not be so upset. Since the age of 18 Lester had always said he would kill himself, though to me this just seemed like another way to get attention.

I cried when I saw Elton John being interviewed by Piers Morgan – and just not because Lester had phoned me up when Piers interviewed Barbara Windsor, full of hate and jealousy and raging that he should have had Piers's show, though he was never willing to put the work and effort into something like that. As Elton described his addiction problems he talked about pushing his friends away in favour of sycophants. Elton said if he had not been taken into rehab he would be dead.

On a pleasant evening out with Lester I got him to agree to go to The Meadows clinic in Arizona, as many people had rated the place. I made the calls and sent all the details in an e-mail to Lester the next day, promising that I would look after his dog while he was away. He never called me back, but two days later called up drunk, saying: 'What the fuck is this e-mail, darling? No way!' Much as I know an addict has to help himself, I wished I could have picked him up by the scruff of the neck and marched him to rehab.

He had been so horrible to his real friends that when he sent us a text message saying 'Love you all' at two in the morning, I just looked at it and went back to sleep. I tried to ring him the next day and eventually heard that he had tried to kill himself, but was now staying with Ingrid Tarrant in the country and she was looking after him. Ingrid is a lovely woman but what Lester really needed was to be locked up in rehab.

I knew that by now he had spent much of his inheritance, mainly on sycophants, coke and drink, but he was still wealthy and apparently surprisingly healthy considering the rock 'n' roll lifestyle he led.

Lester was obsessed with celebrities, no matter how minor. He was constantly making friends with them, mainly as he wanted to be them. When they did not give him a hundred per cent attention he would throw his toys out of the pram and send vile text messages to them. Lovely Zoe Lucker, who was in *Footballers' Wives*, was a great mate but Lester's constant demands on her strained the relationship. So I was worried that it would be the same with Ingrid.

Ingrid was a rock to Lester. A few weeks later she was going to see Vicki Michelle (better known as Yvette in *'Allo 'Allo!*) who was appearing in Guildford in the musical, *Stop Dreamin'*. Lester begged to go too and although Ingrid was not sure he was ready to go out, she gave in. At the after-show party Lester began to drink very heavily and refused to leave. Ingrid was not drinking that night as she was driving and she had to wait in the car for an hour before he appeared.

Lester then demanded a kebab. Ingrid said she had no idea where to get one but, to her dismay, as she turned the corner there was a kebab shop. The whole evening was a disaster, but Ingrid did not give in or throw Lester out, and after a few choice words she went to bed. In the morning she woke to find Lester had driven drunk through the night back to Battersea and had left a note of apology.

He continued to get help from local doctors for his depression, addiction and mental health, and in fact seemed on good form, ringing me to tell me everything that was going on. On the Sunday he finished doing his food run and then picked me up for coffee. 'Anywhere you want to go, darling, I know I have been selfish in the past but this is a new me,' he said.

Of course that lasted about two minutes, as he stipulated it could be anywhere I wanted to go as long as it had heaters outside so we could smoke there. He then went on to tell me all about the 25-year-old straight surfer he had slept with the night before. He seemed to be just fine but maybe it was all a smokescreen as two weeks later he apparently tried to take his life again. Tragically, this time he seemed to have succeeded.

14

A Funeral For a Friend

It was 5.55 in the morning and I was woken by a text on my phone. The caller was Michael Tees, not a long-time friend; in fact, we had met on only a handful of occasions, yet it was Michael who was given the responsibility of breaking the news that my best friend, Lester Middlehurst, had passed away at 4.45 on the morning of 26 November, 2010 after being in a coma for two days.

At first I was horrified that someone I barely knew had broken the news to me, but he was only following instructions and Lester had often lavished love and attention on relative strangers while being cruel to those he really loved. The text took me from great sadness to tears of laughter at the thought, and I'm sure if he were looking down, Lester would have been smirking too.

Also, there was the woman who had apparently put herself in charge of things at the hospital; I had never really liked her, and had always seen her as a bad influence on Lester, not that he needed much encouragement, of course. When she was around we would often hide, pretending we weren't in, or else meet up outside Battersea where she couldn't find us. When she did turn up, often with a few men in tow, Lester would be on the coke and drinking within minutes. During the last two weeks of his life she did step up to help, going round the local bars and asking them not to serve him. But it was too little, too late and I was never entirely sure of her motivation.

It was not long before Pamela Sharrock (the Contessa) called me in tears to break the news. She was speechless that Michael had got to me first and that he had told me by text. Her upset turned to rage at Michael and she had no idea why I was finding it funny. Much as I explained that it was not Michael's fault, she seemed hell bent on having a go at him.

Denise Welch was due to be fronting Lorraine Kelly's show that day and we wanted to stop the news getting to her until after the broadcast. But the minute I tuned in I knew that she had heard. She did not give her usual confident, vibrant performance and seemed preoccupied.

The wonderful Rose Hirst, Lester's cousin (though not a biological one, as Lester had been adopted), was Lester's executor and had travelled down from Alderley Edge in Cheshire. She rang and it was a relief to hear her voice, as she would now take over Lester's affairs and there would be no more calls from people I barely knew.

Lester always had very pragmatic views on death or tragedy. On one of our first ever holidays together, to mainland Greece in 1986, we went to a beach about half an hour outside Athens. It was ten minutes from the gay beach, which Lester had checked out with his Spartacus book (a guide for gay travellers). He would hide the guide in his luggage in case customs found it and discovered he was a homosexual. Even a blind dog would have known that Lester was gay but, much as he was relaxed with friends and in his work environment, he could be odd with others about it. He would ask taxi drivers to take us a street away from a gay club and then we would walk back once the cab had gone so the driver would not think he was gay.

It was a holiday to remember, as we ran out of spending money four days into the two-week break, so I set to work cutting people's hair on the beach or blow-drying for the women in their rooms before they went out for the evening. As I never really sit still on a beach, I really enjoyed it, and it meant we made loads of friends. Lester was my pimp, talking people into haircuts or suggesting they have their hair done for a night out. Ever since the Greek holiday I always take my hair tools with me in case I run short of cash.

From our penthouse suite I could see Lester glistening by the side of the pool, slathered in sun oil and rather resembling a small humpback whale that had washed up on the beach. He had conned the proprietor of the hotel into giving us the penthouse suite at a reduced rate. News came in that our home town of Brighton had been attacked by the IRA and that a bomb had gone off at the Grand Hotel while Margaret Thatcher and her Cabinet were attending the annual Conservative Party conference. There were unconfirmed rumours of deaths and many injured, including journalists. Neither of us had a mobile phone at the time, so I dashed down to the pool to tell Lester and then went to phone home to see what was going on.

Hearing the news, Lester barely lifted his head from his sun lounger. 'Oh, don't ring, darling, what can we do? We can't afford to dash home and if someone is dead or horribly mutilated, they're going to be the same when we get home. When they're dead, they're dead,' he said.

He lay back down, taking in the warm rays and as I walked off he lifted his head: 'I would be upset if Emma (his dog) was having a walk past the Grand and was killed though,' he said. Then he shook his head, remembering that Paul never walked the dog in that direction, lay back down and promptly fell asleep.

Needless to say, I went ahead and called home to get the news and all was fine with our nearest and dearest; I just didn't mention it to Lester. The holiday was not marred by the fact that Lester had taken off for two days with Tommy the Turk, whom he'd met in Omonoia Square in Athens at two o'clock one morning. His addictive appetite for sex meant he often went missing but somehow I knew he was OK and it gave me two days of complete relaxation.

Lester had no religious beliefs and lived for the here and now. He saw death as inconvenient, but whoever it was that had died could be replaced or he could just move on. Except for pets; he was always devastated by their loss. When his third dog died, he ran a bath and got in with a large Cointreau and 12 sleeping pills, and sent a text message to his neighbour, Lesley Goring, the fashion guru, telling her what he had done. But by the time she rushed round he had got out of the bath, dressed and had gone to some friends around the corner who had called with an invite to an impromptu party. Lesley was livid – she's an extremely busy woman, with back-to-back fashion shows to direct, and she had castings in the morning. 'Yeah, I changed my mind,' was Lester's only response. He was like the little boy that cried wolf.

On the night of his actual death, he had been at dinner with Lesley, who, much as she found Lester a royal pain in the bottom, adored having him as her neighbour and the two walked freely between each other's homes, regularly eating together.

Lester had left Lesley's and had agreed to let a friend of hers, 'Whiskers', stay in his spare bedroom. He had obviously decided the night wasn't over, even though everyone else had gone to bed. He took off to a bar for one last drink, but was refused entry and neighbours had heard raised voices. Fuming, he returned home and made himself a cheese sandwich, ran himself a bath in the downstairs bathroom next to the kitchen, and apparently took out three packs of antidepressants and 27 sleeping pills and took the lot.

Lester never made it to the bath; the water was cold when he was found in the morning. Nor did he take himself off to the comfortable sofa in the adjacent living room, but lay down on the kitchen floor. The Contessa and I both thought at the time that he positioned himself there deliberately, so when his overnight guest came down she would find him and call for help. But when he was found it was too late, and despite Lesley trying to revive him, and the paramedics, who battled for an hour and a half, he never came round.

He was taken to St George's Hospital in Tooting and put on life support. If he had regained consciousness the doctors said he would have been a vegetable, something Lester feared more than death itself. So it was better that he slipped away quietly.

My emotions were so up and down. Part of me was really angry with him; he had money and could have sold his place in Battersea and moved somewhere with fewer temptations and bad influences. But the lure of the bars and restaurants was too strong. Most therapists say that moving does not help addiction problems, as your addictions will find you wherever you are unless you confront them and get treatment. But in a different place Lester might have had more of a chance – when sitting in watching television or a DVD he never wanted a drink. But he found it impossible to walk past the Square with its bars and see a familiar face and not sit down and have a quick drink to catch up with the gossip. That quick drink would find him, nine hours later, crawling home drunk and coked out of his head. Then he would collapse into bed, with the comfort of sleeping pills that he kept on his bedside table.

Denise and the Contessa went to view his body. I could not bring myself to go and see him, preferring to remember the good times. The Contessa rang an hour later, in a lighter mood. 'He looked so peaceful and had a little smirk on his face,' she said, and then laughed – Lester was the only person who seemed to have got fatter after he died! Lester's horrific diet, with full-fat everything and chocolate éclairs, used to leave us speechless.

The week after he died, Jane Moore, Chris Day (a.k.a. Podge, the former manager of Soho House), the Contessa, cousin Rose and I all met to sort out his clothes, which we were donating to a local animal charity shop. I was given the job of picking an outfit for him to wear on the day of the funeral.

It took time to choose the right look, but I came across the perfect jacket. When I was cleaning out the pockets, I discovered a packet of cocaine – how very Lester! I showed it to everyone and it broke the sadness; we all fell about laughing and briefly toyed with the idea of burying it with him, in case he wanted to party on the way. But instead we opted to send him off with a pack of 20 Consulates and a lighter so he could have a fag on the way to heaven.

Before the funeral we met at Lester's house again. There we were joined by his long-term friend Mark Haddigan, who played Timothy Able in *The Bill*, and Ingrid Tarrant arrived with champagne. Denise was there early on and looked stunning in black. We all set off more or less at the same time to the crematorium, but the traffic was heavy and, though it was only in Tooting, quite a few of us got lost.

It was my first time as pallbearer, and as we also had taken a wrong turn, making us late, Martin and I arrived with only seconds to spare. I was bursting for the little boy's room, but there was no time for that. I had to lift the coffin, taking the back together with Paul Cooper, as we were the tallest. Podge was at the front. Suddenly I became overwhelmed with sadness at the thought that I was carrying the body of my dearest friend. I couldn't hear a word the undertaker was saying and, being accident prone, I was convinced I would trip up and send Lester's body flying into the assembled mourners. It was a relief when we finally set the coffin down and I took my seat in the front row, unaware that many of the most important people in Lester's life were missing.

The funeral was a travesty. *Funeral Blues* by W H Auden, which featured in *Four Weddings and a Funeral*, was read quite inappropriately by a relation, not a lover, though Rose read a beautiful poem about a bear called Lester. Podge read a lovely eulogy, though it mainly took in Lester's party days and missed out his wonderful journalistic career and charity work; really, I should have covered that section, but I just felt too overwhelmed to speak. Podge recounted that when Lester was once asked what he would do if Podge died, Lester calmly replied: 'Sad for a second and then get a new friend.'

Blood Brothers star, Keith Burns, had been scheduled to sing, but he found it too distressing to perform and the Contessa's daughter, Tilly, had agreed to stand in. But she was nowhere to be found so we all sang the song very badly and Rose wisely cut it short, and then Lester's body was cremated.

It takes less time to cremate a body than it does to get a pizza delivered. We had the 2pm slot, and there was another funeral party waiting outside for 2.30pm, so we all had to be out.

There were some very upset people outside – Pam, the Contessa, ran up to me, hysterical. Her children, Tilly and Wills (who was also supposed to be a pallbearer) together with Denise and another long-standing friend, Samantha Kenwright, had missed the funeral altogether as they got lost. Tilly had collapsed as she reached the door of the crematorium and heard the final music, realising that they had missed it all.

There were lots of people from the past, and it was beautiful to see how many had turned out. Perhaps if Lester had known how many people loved him, it might have made a difference, but in my heart I do not think it would have changed anything. I don't think there was ever enough love to make him truly happy.

Billy Murray and his wife Elaine were among the first to come up to me. Lester and I had enjoyed many a good night out with them and I looked after Billy's press for him a while back. Gary Webster and his wife, Wendy Turner, were good friends to both

Lester and me, and Nicola Duffett, the former *EastEnders* actress, was also there. Nicola brightens up even the saddest occasion but this time she had tears in her eyes.

There was great confusion about the day; originally it was going to be by invite only but when details were published in the *Daily Mail* saying 'family and close friends only' it opened the floodgates. Lester made everyone feel like a close friend, from dog walkers to Albanian cleaning ladies, not to mention celebrities, even if he'd only met them once. He often kept friends separate, and with so little time on our hands to give out the invites, some people were offended that we had not issued them with personal invitations. But we were pleased to see them.

Denise saw the funny side. Lester, being Machiavellian, had often caused problems among his friends simply to amuse himself, and in death it was no different. He would surely have been laughing away at the confusion.

We held the party at the Landor Theatre pub. Lester hated the word wake so we were calling it a celebration of life. Guests were treated to Kir Royale, one of Lester's favourite tipples. The luxury nibbles that Lester always obsessed about at any event or party that he gave were sadly missing, apparently cancelled by one of the organisers.

It was truly fascinating to hear some people reinvent their relationship with him. They made him sound like a demigod, rather than someone they might regularly have threatened to throttle. One distant person, whose husband Lester had taken to bed thus ruining her marriage, seemed to completely forget the incident, and was in floods of tears throughout the day. As in life, Lester could get away with the sort of behaviour mere mortals would never be forgiven for.

Lester had caused so much trouble among Denise's family, though, and they stayed away. Annie, Denise's mum, did not want anything to do with him after Lester had caused such a rift between Denise and her sister, Debbie. Matthew (Denise's son) was recording that day and Denise's husband, Tim, was recording the TV series *Benidorm* in Spain.

There were warring sections at the celebrations; some of the newer friends had a go at long-term friends for not inviting people we barely knew about. Denise and I knocked back gallons of Kir Royale and got plastered in true Lester fashion! Denise made it to bed at around three in the morning and I wasn't that much earlier. It was exactly as our dear friend would have wanted – chaotic, some celebrities, a few rows and some bad behaviour followed by a very late night!

If any good came of it, then it was that our small group that had started in Brighton became even closer. We would make more of an effort to see each other in the months ahead, but it was the end of an era. No matter what, Lester would never be forgotten.

15

Ice Queens and a Twist

True to form, there was a twist to Lester's death. When the inquest was held at Westminster Coroner's Court on 17 February, 2011, it turned out that the concerns the Contessa and I had over his death were well founded. Lester had not, in fact, taken his life and the coroner's verdict was that he had died of natural causes due to hypoxic brain damage.

Unknown to Lester, he was suffering from an enlarged heart and fatty liver, due in part to his lifestyle and alcohol consumption of as much as 350 units a week. He had suffered a massive heart attack on the night of his death, which was the reason he had not gone to the sofa to lie down or got into the bath that he had run. He had suffered from diffuse brain swelling as a result of oxygen deprivation.

It was hard to hear at the inquest that he was lonely and desperate for a partner, drinking a bottle of Cointreau a night, plus wine, and how his cocaine abuse and sleeping pill addiction counteracted his antidepressant medication, something I had been nagging him about for ages. On the upside, the coroner said he sounded like a wonderful man and a real character; he was hailed a showbiz legend.

How did we all get it so wrong? It was just that Lester was the little boy who cried wolf. Everyone simply assumed when he was found that it was another attempt to take his life and of course a suicide note had been found. But it turned out to be an old note from one of his previous attempts – it was found upstairs and taken down to the kitchen by a friend who neglected to say where she had found it originally. The empty medication boxes that had also led us to believe it was suicide turned out to just be old packets. The post-mortem revealed that all Lester had in him that night was some ibuprofen.

The knowledge that he had not, in fact, taken his life, made it easier for his friends. Lester was never going to be an old soul and during his time on earth his larger than life character brought plenty of laughter and joy. If he was looking down on us all at the funeral, I'm sure he'd have been in convulsions of laughter. 'You stupid lot; I didn't top myself, I had a heart attack,' he'd be screaming, as he took another sip of chilled Cointreau.

These days I still get my scissors out from time to time, as I've kept on a few special clients. Although I dearly loved my days of session work, and miss it sometimes, it's a relief not to be lugging two huge bags around London all the time. Freelance writing can be lonely at times and not interacting with people on a daily basis can have its downside. But I guess my drama teacher, Michael Wilcox, was right – I did get bored with hairdressing in the end, though it took quite a time for me to tire of it.

As I say, after Lester's death, we all made an effort to see each other as much as we could. Denise had taken on *Dancing on Ice*, which meant she was in London more often and we would meet for dinner. We're a bad influence on each other, though – we went out one night for a quick pizza at six o'clock and by midnight Denise was gently enquiring how we'd ended up at the home of my gay porn star neighbour, Miles Bentley. She did show pictures of him to all the *Loose Women* presenters and the gay crew and we all had a great time.

The Contessa, Pam Sharrock, moved to the country and is

running a new retreat hotel (Flore Retreat, in Northamptonshire), specialising in well-being. 'It's not a spa hotel,' she keeps telling us, but as long as it has a bar, we'll have plenty of well-being! With the Contessa at the helm it should be a huge success, and will doubtless become a big hit with the celebrity set.

Rose Hirst works as a theatrical agent for Pemberton Associates and has moved to Alderley Edge, minutes from Denise's home. After IVF treatment, she gave birth to a beautiful little boy, Harrison, who is now ten years old, and this summer she'll be getting married.

Jane Moore released her latest book – *Love Is On The Air* – in February 2011, and she and husband, Gary Farrow, have a five-year-old daughter, Grace. Jane's oldest daughter, Ellie, is 18 and stunning and studies at Manchester University. Jane writes a weekly column for *The Sun* and also for *GQ*, and appears regularly on television.

We plan a memorial for Lester in the winter, and we want it to be a real humdinger of a send-off. As I got ready one evening to see Denise in *Dancing on Ice*, I thought how much he would have loved hanging out with all the celebrities, and the inevitable phone calls the next day, chortling over the mischief he'd have created and all the new best friends he'd have made.

People who win tickets to see the *Dancing on Ice* 'Live Show' should proceed with caution, however. My advice would be to stay at home, buy a bottle of bubbly and watch it on the TV; it'll be far more fun.

Early on Sunday afternoon I caught the train from Clapham to Cobham with theatre producer Tom Hopkins. It was a wet, cold day and we were both hungover, but very happy to support Denise as she stepped out on the ice to perform her first routine with hunky dance partner, Matt Evers. Denise was convinced she would not make it to the final line-up so wanted me to come in case it was her last performance as, in her own words, 'a professional ice-skater'.

Denise was already talking about doing the touring version, not so much for her own sake but because she knew that Matt did not earn much money from the television show. In contrast, the touring version, owned by Torvill and Dean, was first class all the way for the celebrities and the professional skaters.

Ingrid Tarrant picked us up in Cobham and was taking us to Shepperton Studios in Middlesex. We weren't quite sure how to get there and worried we'd be late but, after a lot of twiddling with the sat nav, we made it in the nick of time.

The security guys at the studios, once they realised we were on one of the stars' guest lists, seemed unsure whether to give us directions or break into a song from *The Sound of Music*. Instead they gave us wristbands, insisting we put them on before we drove off, and wishing us a good evening.

It was a good hike from the car park and Ingrid's hair was getting wet, so we made a dash for the welcome bar. We queued up again to get into the bar, where we were given another wristband to prove we were legitimate guests. By this time I wasn't sure whether I was going to see a show or have a medical…There was barely time for a quick, cheap – but not free – glass of wine when security shouted for us to come to the studio. The wristbands were checked and we all began to feel rather like cattle.

We had to wait in line to enter the studio, in the rain, for almost half an hour, after which some jobsworth checked our wristbands yet again. They were colour-coded and my blue one meant I would be sitting in the area designated for Denise's friends and the cameras would know where we were sitting so they could get our reactions when she performed.

Despite all the waiting, it was a great evening and a real get-together. Denise's whole family were there: husband, Tim Healy; her rock band singer son, Matt, who fronts the band Big Sleep;

and Louis, their youngest, full of energy and marvelling at all the beautiful girls. Looking fitter and more glamorous than ever despite fighting cancer was Denise's mum, Annie. Debbie, Denise's sister, was also there with her beautiful kids.

It was great to see them all, so I stopped moaning and we all took our seats. It was still only 5.30pm though, and we had an hour to wait until the show began. The aisles were patrolled by a mini-army of women with clipboards, and you got the distinct impression one of these clipboard Nazis would shoot if you tried to move.

Once the show started, it was as *Will and Grace* star Leslie Jordan described it – a nancy boy's dream sequence, all glitz and with a wicked queen in the form of judge, Jason Gardiner. Denise was last on and, wearing an amazing wig, danced to 'Pack Up' by Eliza Doolittle. Unbeknown to me, Denise could see me on the screen backstage and said I looked like a worried mother waiting for her child to come on stage at her first school play. She and Matt thought that was very funny, apparently. When she did come on the girl did good, though Jason said it was like Matt dancing with his mum. But Denise admits it got her the mum and 'cougar' vote in a backlash against his ageist comment.

Denise loves gay men and always gave Jason the benefit of the doubt, saying he was just being a panto character. But by the end of the show she really disliked Jason. I think she would have punched him given half a chance for the things he said about her and husband Tim. After this, Denise didn't have a good word to say about him; I had never heard her use the word queen before, but she does now when it comes to Jason. I have no idea why a dancer who is not a professional skater is even judging the show.

We were let out to the toilets at the interval and given a sugar doughnut but we were kept caged so there was no danger of anyone leaving or escaping to the bar. By this time we were so hungry that Ingrid and I ate two doughnuts each and caught up on the gossip.

Denise got into the final line-up so it was back to the bar for some more cheap wine once it was all over. Denise arrived to loud cheers and was exhausted but lapping up every minute of the excitement. When she introduced me to the senior producer of the series, Michelle Langer, we both stopped in our tracks – we had been on holiday together some years before in Spain, along with Lester and Anne Shooter, another *Daily Mail* journalist.

I regaled Denise and the gang with the story of how we had taken out a four-person pedalo with a slide on it, Anne and I pedalling as Lester sunbathed and Michelle chatted. When Michelle and Lester decided to cool off and have a swim, Anne and I began to think we were getting a raw deal but I would never have trusted Lester with any mode of transport, even a pedalo.

Suddenly I spied a giant Portuguese man-of-war near the pedalo and shouted to Lester and Michelle to get out of the water. Lester assumed I was joking but eventually spotted it. Well, he could have won an Olympic swimming medal with the speed with which he returned to the pedalo. Michelle got there at the same time and, the age of chivalry being long dead in Lester's world, he pushed her under the water to get up the ladder first.

Michelle and I laughed as we remembered Lester getting on the boat and screaming, 'PEDAL FAST', as if the jellyfish was going to eat the pedalo. Michelle must be a real stickler for discipline on the set, because Denise told everyone I met from the show that I had gone on holiday with Michelle, and they were all shocked, as though they couldn't imagine her enjoying herself. Take it from me, though, Michelle sure was a fun holiday companion.

We stayed far too late and I missed the last train back to

London, so I stayed at Ingrid's place in Cobham. Her home was stunning and there were so many rooms you could get lost in it. We cracked open a bottle of bubbly even though it was late, and we chatted about us both writing. I told her the downside of writing was that everyone thinks you are going to write about them. I told her the story of when I was invited to a party being held for the lovely Michelle Collins at one of her friends' homes. I went with the singer Rose-Marie, and we'd been there around ten minutes when Michelle's over-protective mother asked me to leave because I was a journalist. I promised I was not that kind of writer but she spat back: 'If you lie down with dogs you're bound to pick up fleas.' Michelle was livid with her mum, who did not get her way, because I stayed. You're not as welcome as a journalist as you are when you're a celebrity hairdresser, but the quote did make me laugh.

We talked a lot about Lester and how Ingrid had tried to help him. Before we knew it, it was 3.30am and I needed to be up for seven to head back to London for a ten o'clock appointment. I woke up in time, but the heavens had opened and Ingrid drove me to the station, barely able to see through her windscreen.

The rain poured down the train window and the morning commuters crammed into the carriage looked so tired and grey. At every station, I looked up from my copy of *Metro* to see wet, miserable bodies piling in. As I did, a shudder went through me. I was back in the place of so many terrible memories – Surbiton. Then I smiled. Maybe without those memories my life would not have been so diverse, driven, rich and exciting; or so full of people I never dreamed of meeting back in the days of my suburban nightmare; people who were now my friends and accepted me for who I am.